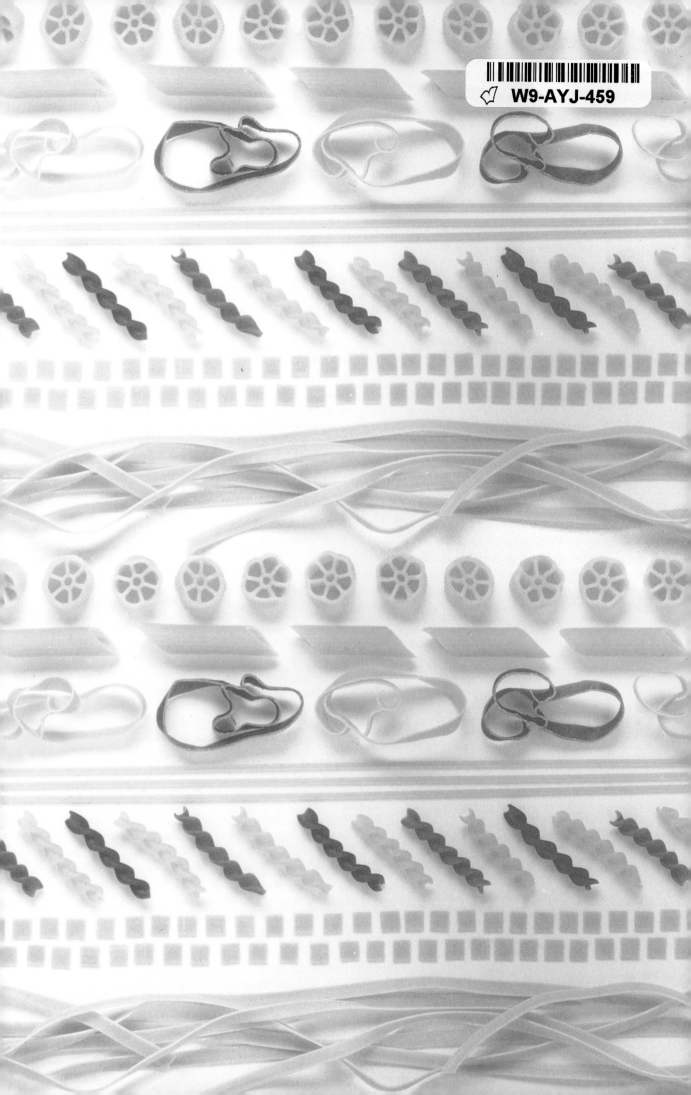

THE
CLASSIC
PASTA
COOKBOOK

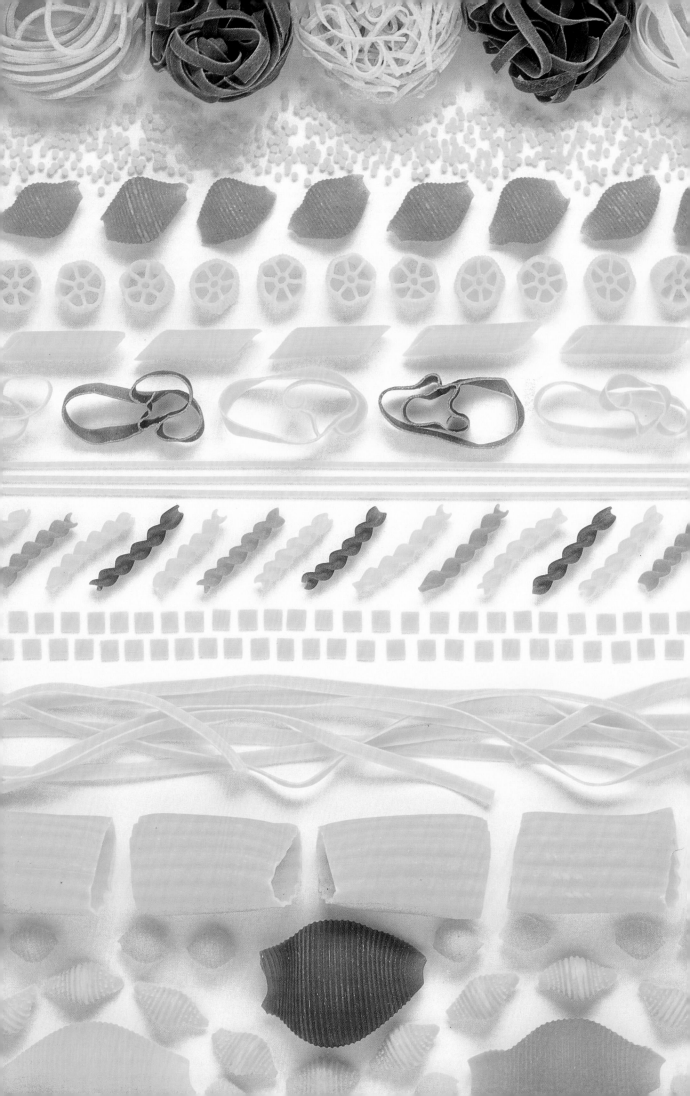

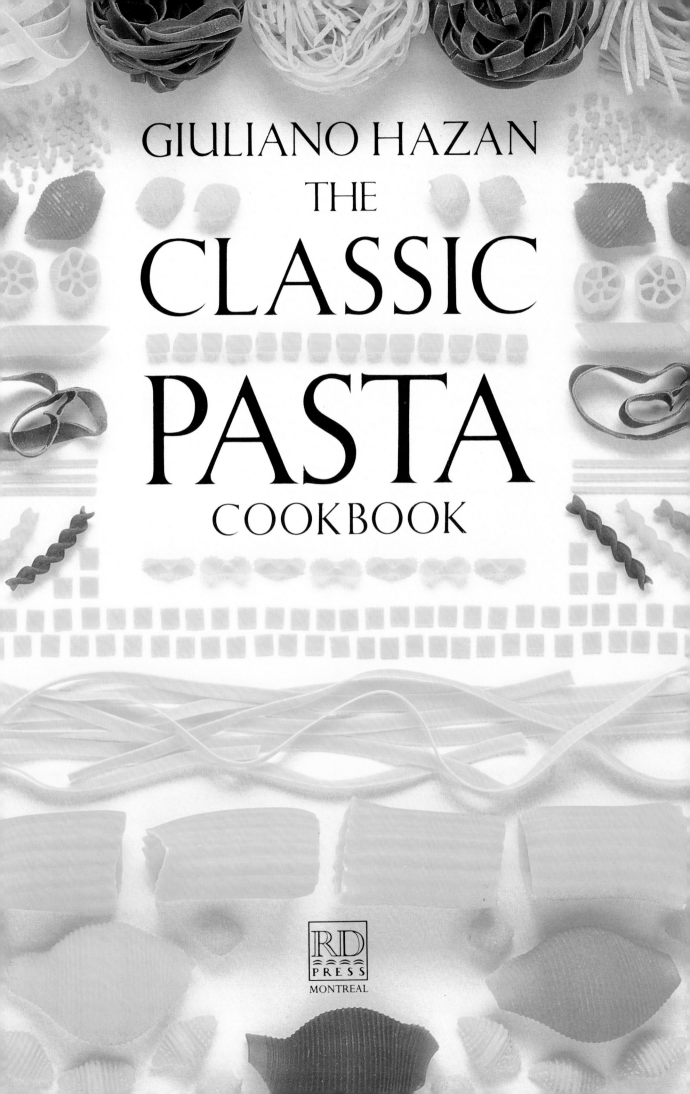

GIULIANO HAZAN

THE
CLASSIC
PASTA
COOKBOOK

RD
PRESS
MONTREAL

A DORLING KINDERSLEY BOOK

Project Editor
Mari Roberts

Art Editor
Tracey Clarke

Senior Editor
Carolyn Ryden

Managing Editor
Daphne Razazan

Managing Art Editor
Carole Ash

US Editor
Jeanette Mall

Photography
Amanda Heywood
Clive Streeter

Production
Antony Heller

A mia mamma, con tanto amore

Published in Canada in 1993 by
The Reader's Digest Association (Canada) Ltd.
215 Redfern Avenue, Westmount, Quebec H3Z 2V9

The Reader's Digest Association (Canada) Ltd.
is a licensed user of the trademark RD Press.

First published in Great Britain in 1993
by Dorling Kindersley Limited,
9 Henrietta Street, London WC2E 8PS

CANADIAN CATALOGUING-IN-PUBLICATION DATA
Hazan, Giuliano
  The classic pasta cookbook : a comprehensive guide to
Italian pasta with over 100 authentic recipes

1st Canadian ed.
Includes index.
ISBN 0-88850-308-3

  1. Cookery (Pasta). 2. Cookery, Italian. I.
Reader's Digest Association (Canada).
II. Title.

TX809.M17H39 1993   641.8'22   C93-090184-3

Reproduced in Singapore by Colourscan
Printed and bound in Italy by A. Mondadori Editore, Verona

95 96 97 / 5 4

CONTENTS

FOREWORD 6
by Marcella Hazan

INTRODUCTION 8

A CATALOG OF PASTA

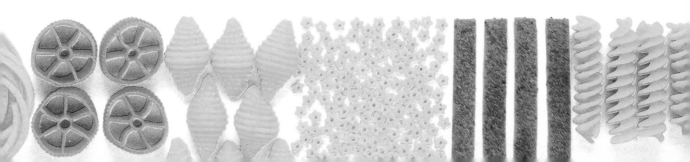

FOREWORD

I t is not every day that a mother has the opportunity to introduce her son to his readers. When it happens, she should take advantage of her unique knowledge of the aptitudes and experiences that have led the author to his calling. She should start at the very beginning, which is what I propose to do.

Giuliano's passion for pasta sprang to life fully formed one day at dinner when he was three. It was the first time an adult dish of pasta had been put before him, and I well remember what it was: handmade *tortelloni* his grandmother had prepared, stuffed with *ricotta* and Swiss chard. Without ever coming up for air, he put away a portion that might have strained the capacity of a full-grown man, and as he finished he fell instantly asleep. He came out of his stupor a confirmed devotee of pasta, a devotion he has fed, and which has fed him, from that day to this.

Very early on, Giuliano's aptitude for consuming pasta began to coincide with an interest in producing it. The kitchen was his favorite playroom. He was chopping onions as soon as his hands could firmly hold a knife, and stirring sauce as soon as he was tall enough to look into the saucepan on the range. As he grew, to cook became as commonplace for him as to throw a ball was for other boys.

He would not be unwilling, I am sure, to acknowledge his debt to the Hazan kitchen, where the recipes constantly being tested provided his talents with the most favorable ground on which to develop. But the debt does not fall entirely on his side. The published form of many of those recipes owes much to his palate, often pressed into service as the official tasting instrument. To those who have not observed Giuliano at work, I can only describe his palate as possessing the gastronomic equivalent of perfect pitch.

As you look through and cook from the recipes he has set down here you will see what I mean. The judiciously balanced flavors of his sauces, his light-handed way with herbs and condiments, the illuminating pairing of sauce with the most congenial shape and type of pasta, all show an extraordinary commitment to and command of those principles of cooking whose sole aim is to produce satisfying flavor. You will never find Giuliano asking himself what he can do that is different but, rather, what he can do that tastes good.

In my life as a cook, both before it became my profession and since, I have always learned most about cooking from those who took it up out of irresistible love. This book is the product of just such love. Any cook using it will be deliciously rewarded. As a matter of fact, there are a number of things I am myself longing to try. *Bravo Giuliano!*

INTRODUCTION

For me, few foods can compete with the satisfaction and pleasure of eating a good dish of pasta. It is difficult to imagine many Italians surviving without it. In fact, when the first Italian immigrants began arriving in North America at the end of the 19th century, ships from southern Italy laden with pasta soon followed them. By 1913 almost 700,000 tons were being exported to the New World.

Food historians have long debated the origin of pasta. Marco Polo has been attributed with discovering it in China and bringing it back to Italy in 1295, but Italian historians claim pasta was known and used in Italy before Marco Polo was even born. Sicilians say they invented it, and provide references to "macarruni" in literature as proof, while a late 19th-century Neapolitan writer, Matilde Serao, tells of a fable that attempts to designate Naples as the place where pasta made its first appearance.

She wrote that in 1220 there lived in Naples a magician called Chico. He rarely came out of his top-floor rooms except for occasional trips to the market to buy various herbs and tomatoes. (Getting tomatoes was a neat trick for Chico to pull because everybody else in Europe had to wait another 400 years, until well after Europeans first went to America.) He spent his days in front of a bubbling cauldron, and his nights poring over ancient texts and manuscripts. After many years, he achieved his goal. He rejoiced in the knowledge that he had discovered something that would contribute to the happiness of all people.

During all this time, Jovanella, whose husband worked in the kitchens of the King's palace, had been spying on Chico's every move from her balcony, which gave her a view of his rooms. When she finally discovered his secret, she told her husband, "Go tell the

King's chef that I have discovered a new food so exquisite that it deserves to be tasted by His Majesty." So her husband spoke to the chef, who spoke to the butler, who spoke to a count, who, after much deliberation, spoke to His Majesty. The King, who was getting bored with his food, welcomed the opportunity to try something different. Jovanella was admitted to the royal kitchens and began to prepare what she had seen the magician create.

She combined flour, water and eggs to form a dough, which she then painstakingly rolled out until it was as thin as parchment. She cut it into strips and formed rings, which she left out to dry. She then cooked onions, meat and tomatoes over a very low heat for a long time until they formed a sauce. When it was time to eat, she cooked the pasta in boiling water, drained it, then tossed it with the sauce and "the famous cheese from Parma." The King was so impressed by what she had made that he asked her how she had managed to invent such a remarkable thing. She answered that an angel had revealed it to her in a dream. The King ordered that she be rewarded handsomely for having made such an important contribution to human happiness. One day Chico smelled the aroma of his wonderful invention coming from a nearby house. Incredulous, he asked what was being prepared. He was told of a wonderful new food that an angel had revealed to a woman in her sleep. Heartbroken, he ran off and was never seen again.

However it may first have appeared, Italians have been making pasta for centuries. Although it has evolved into many different shapes, the basic ingredients are still the same. There are two main categories: flour-and-water pasta and egg pasta. It is important to understand the characteristics of each.

Flour-and-water pasta uses flour made from durum (hard) wheat, a high-gluten flour called *semolina* in Italian. This category includes packaged pastas such as *spaghetti*, tubes, and many special shapes. They are sturdy and work well with spicy, zesty sauces and with olive oil-based ones. This pasta is referred to as store-bought pasta and it is best when factory-made. Industrial-strength machines are necessary to knead the hard dough, and humidity- and temperature-controlled chambers are required to dry the final shapes so they will not crack and break when cooked. I do not know of any brands made outside Italy that can match the quality of the Italian-made flour-and-water pastas.

The other category of pasta is made with flour and eggs; it is usually referred to as homemade egg pasta or simply homemade pasta, although it is often (and inappropriately) known as "fresh pasta." It is made with a soft-wheat flour known in Italy as "00" that is roughly equivalent to plain or all-purpose flour. The recipe for the dough varies slightly depending on the region. For example, in Tuscany, some olive oil and salt are added, and in Liguria a little water is used. But in Emilia-Romagna, which is known for producing the finest homemade pasta and is the birthplace of *tagliatelle, tagliolini, lasagne,* and several stuffed pastas, the dough is made using only flour and eggs and nothing else (except for spinach or tomato pasta). Egg pasta absorbs sauces more readily than flour-and-water store-bought pasta, and so is well suited to butter- and cream-based sauces, and to milder sauces that match its delicate texture. With sauces where olive oil is prominent, egg pasta would absorb too much oil and become slick and gummy.

Egg pasta, unlike store-bought pasta, should be made at home. The finest homemade pasta is porous, delicately textured, and very thin, a result that can be achieved only by kneading the dough by hand and thinning it out with a rolling pin. Very good egg pasta can also be produced by rolling it through a machine if you are willing to sacrifice some of its porousness and texture. Kneading should always be done by hand. The so-called "fresh" pasta found in the refrigerator compartments of supermarkets and speciality shops is egg pasta at its worst. The noodles are usually too thick, the dough is made with *semolina*, which is much too hard a flour for egg pasta, and it is refrigerated so that it can be called "fresh." Cold is pasta's greatest enemy. In fact, you should avoid cold ingredients or cold surfaces when making it, and the best way to store it is to let it dry completely and then keep it at room temperature. It is of no importance whether pasta is "fresh" or not. There is no discernible difference between pasta used immediately after it is made, while still moist, and pasta that has dried completely and been stored for several weeks. If you must buy egg pasta, look for packaged noodles that have been dried and curled into nests and check the ingredients to make sure they are made with eggs.

One of the hardest things for someone who has not grown up eating pasta in Italy is to develop the sensitivity needed to match pastas correctly with sauces. It is also one of the hardest things about pasta to try to explain. It is not a question of mere authenticity, but of attaining the best complement of flavor and texture. The same sauce can result in a mediocre dish or a fabulous dish depending on which type and shape of pasta is used. Use the recipes in this book with the pasta that is indicated or with one of the alternatives, if there are any, at the end of each recipe. This will soon train your palate to know instinctively which pasta is best suited to which sauce.

I hope this book will clear up any misconceptions about Italian pasta and provide you with the fundamental notions needed to prepare, serve, and enjoy one of the greatest foods ever created. *Buon appetito*!

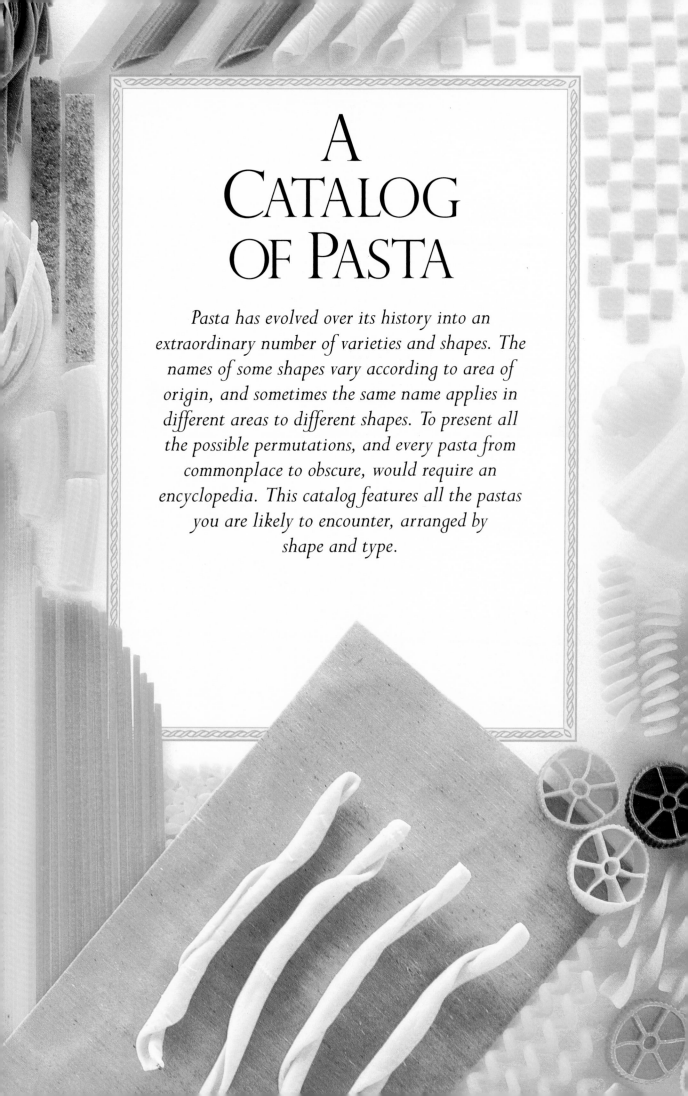

A CATALOG OF PASTA

Pasta has evolved over its history into an extraordinary number of varieties and shapes. The names of some shapes vary according to area of origin, and sometimes the same name applies in different areas to different shapes. To present all the possible permutations, and every pasta from commonplace to obscure, would require an encyclopedia. This catalog features all the pastas you are likely to encounter, arranged by shape and type.

PASTA LUNGA
Long Pasta

All pasta shapes are either long or short. The long shapes illustrated here are the dried, commercially made, flour-and-water pastas. Except for *fusilli*, these pastas are better suited to olive oil and tomato sauces than to sauces with large chunks of vegetables or meat. A good guideline is whether all the ingredients of the sauce will cling together with the long pasta when it is twirled on to a fork.

SPAGHETTI
Probably the best known of all pastas, spaghetti are a masterful invention. Their sturdy texture makes them a perfect vehicle for a wide variety of sauces.

Wholewheat, tomato, and spinach spaghetti

Plain spaghetti

CAPELLI D'ANGELO
The name means "angel hair," and this pasta is good with broth or, if homemade with eggs, makes a wonderful dessert (see page 148). It is never served with a sauce.

SPAGHETTINI
The ini at the end of the word means small, so these are "thin spaghetti." Their delicate shape makes them ideal for light and spicy sauces.

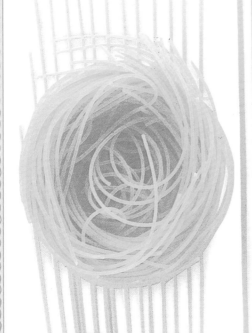

SAUCE SUGGESTIONS

Spaghetti are also perfect for seafood sauces, such as *frutti di mare* (page 78), shrimp (page 74), or mussels (page 81). Or try *bucatini* with a tomato sauce from pages 84–85.

Spaghettini alle erbe (page 72)

Spaghetti alla carbonara (page 66)

Fusilli lunghi alla rustica (page 76)

LINGUINE
Their name means "tongues" and their flat, slippery shape is far more popular outside Italy than within it. In Italy you will find linguine only in a few areas of the south.

Bucatini

BUCATINI
Also called perciatelli, *these spaghetti-with-a-hole (like thin drinking straws) are wonderful with the robust sauces found in south-central Italy. Bucatoni are slightly fatter than* bucatini.

Bucatoni

FUSILLI LUNGHI
These are "long springs," like telephone cords. They are good with chunky sauces, which cling well to the curves in the pasta.

FETTUCCE

Ribbons

This is the most popular type of homemade egg pasta, which is at its best when rolled out by hand, resulting in a delicate, textured, porous pasta that absorbs and attracts butter- and cream-based sauces like no other. Machine-rolled egg pasta also produces a very good result, although it cannot match hand-rolled. If you must use a store-bought egg pasta, buy only the dried version. "Fresh" egg pasta is usually of such poor quality that it is a waste of time, money, and sauce.

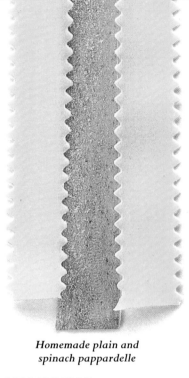

Homemade plain and spinach pappardelle

TAGLIATELLE
Bologna is the home of tagliatelle, and the Bolognese have gone as far as to cast in gold the perfect tagliatella and display it in the Chamber of Commerce. Its most classic match is with meat Bolognese sauce (see page 62).

Homemade plain tagliatelle, straight and in a nest

PAPPARDELLE
In Bologna, these are also called larghissime, which means "very wide." They are the widest ribbon and can be cut either straight or saw-edged.

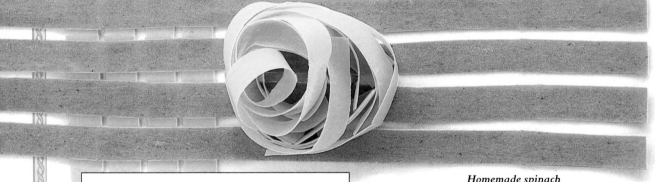

Homemade spinach tagliatelle

RIBBON PASTA WIDTHS

Approximate sizes

Tonnarelli ¹⁄₁₆ in square	
Tagliolini ¹⁄₁₂ in	
Fettuccine / trenette ⅛ in	
Tagliatelle ⅓ in	
Pappardelle ¾ in	

PIZZOCCHERI
This pasta is made with eggs and a combination of plain and buckwheat flour. It is a speciality of the Valtellina region in Lombardy, on the Swiss border.

SAUCE SUGGESTIONS

For an unusual dish, try *fettuccine* with white truffles or orange and mint (page 94) or with lemon (page 96), or *tonnarelli* with melon (page 106).

Pappardelle coi fegatini di pollo (page 102)

Fettuccine all'Alfredo (page 64)

Tonnarelli al melone (page 106)

TONNARELLI

This pasta, whose shape resembles square spaghetti, originated in Abruzzi where it is called maccheroni alla chitarra. Chitarra means "guitar," and the pasta was so named because it was made by pressing a thick sheet of pasta with a rolling pin through the taut wire strings of a guitar-like tool.

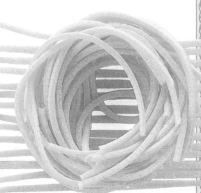

Homemade fettuccine with nests of the store-bought, dried version

Plain tonnarelli, straight and in a nest

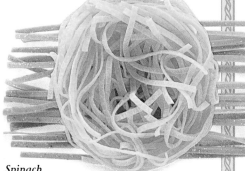

Spinach tagliolini

Plain tagliolini in a nest

FETTUCCINE

Also called trenette, *and probably the best known of the ribbon pastas. It is narrower than* tagliatelle *and more suited to delicate cream-based sauces.*

TAGLIOLINI

This is one of the narrowest of the ribbons. It is occasionally served with a sauce but more commonly with broth.

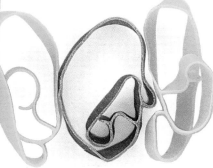

PAGLIA E FIENO

The combination of green (spinach) and yellow (plain egg) fettuccine, cooked and served together, is called paglia e fieno, or "straw and hay."

TUBI

Tubes

Tubular pastas are sturdy, very satisfying, and go well with a variety of sauces. The cavities, especially of the larger tubes, are ideal for trapping chunks in sauces. Their versatility is such that they are one of the few flour-and-water, store-bought pastas that go well with cream sauces. There are a great many sizes of tubes – some so large, such as *gigantoni* (page 21), that you cannot toss them with a sauce and can use them only for baking.

PENNE

These are probably the most widely used of the tubular pastas. Their name means "pens," referring to their pointed, nib-shaped ends. They are available either smooth (lisce) or ridged (rigate) and in a variety of sizes. Penne ziti are fatter than regular penne. Pennoni ("fat" penne) are the largest and the least common.

Penne lisce

Plain and spinach penne rigate

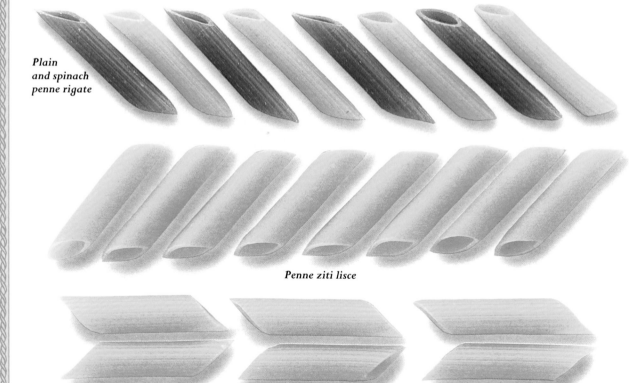

Penne ziti lisce

Penne ziti rigate

Pennoni lisci

Pennoni rigati

SAUCE SUGGESTIONS

Small tubes are good for vegetable sauces, such as cauliflower and cream (page 108), and some meat sauces, such as chicken (page 112) or sausage (page 116).

Penne all'arrabbiata
(page 56)

Garganelli al prosciutto e asparagi
(see Fettuccine, page 95)

Cavatappi alla boscaiola
(page 110)

GARGANELLI
This is the only tube that is made by hand from egg pasta (see page 41 for instructions).

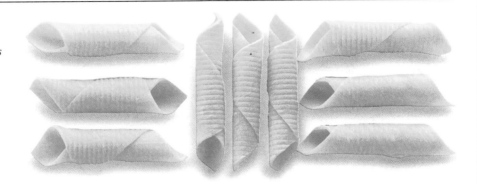

ELICOIDALI
The name means "helixes," and these are straight-edged tubes with ridges that curve around them. They can be used almost interchangeably with rigatoni *(see page 21), although they are narrower.*

CAVATAPPI
These are "corkscrews" and they are like an enlarged section of the long fusilli *(see page 15). They are fun to eat and their twisted shape holds sauces wonderfully.*

TUBI
Tubes

MACCHERONI

This name was synonymous with pasta when it first made an appearance in the aristocratic courts of southern Italy. Now maccheroni *is a general term that can be applied to a variety of tubular pastas. Boccolotti and* chifferi *are mostly used in soups or with butter and cheese for small children. Denti d'elefante, which means "elephant's teeth," and the other two* maccheroni *shown are variations on the basic tube. The* chifferi, *below, are also called* gomiti, *or "elbow" pasta, because of their bent shape.*

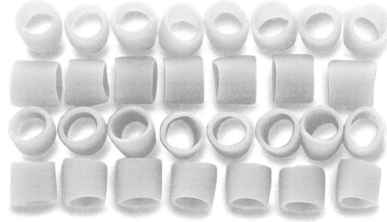

Boccolotti

Maccheroni lisci

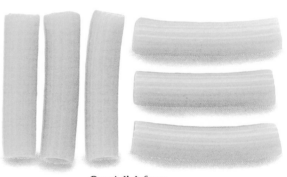

Denti d'elefante

Maccheroni rigati

Chifferi lisci

Chifferi rigati

Larger tubes are ideal for meat sauces. You can also enjoy them with the *pappardelle* sauces, squab (pigeon) or chicken livers, on page 102.

Maccheroni alla salsiccia e ricotta (page 117)

Rigatoni al ragù di agnello (page 114)

Millerighe al coniglio (see Pappardelle, page 103)

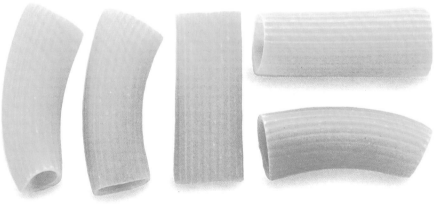

RIGATONI

These large, chewy, and satisfying tubes are a classic and popular shape in Italy. They are excellent with meat sauces or simply tossed with butter, parmigiano-reggiano cheese, and a little cream.

MILLERIGHE

The name means "thousand lines" because of the many ridges on their surface. They are similar to rigatoni *except that they are straight, not slightly curved.*

GIGANTONI

Giganti *is Italian for "giants" and the* oni *ending denotes "extra large," so these are "super-giants." They are too large to eat tossed with a sauce, but are well suited for baked dishes.*

FORME SPECIALI
Special Shapes

Italian pasta-makers have created an immense variety of special pasta shapes. New shapes are being invented all the time, but the traditional shapes tend to predominate. There is no shape, however, whose sole purpose is to be pleasing to the eye: each shape produces a particular sensation on the palate and is best suited to a particular type of sauce. Many of the special shapes pictured here are perfect for sauces with chunks of vegetables or meat because the folds and cavities hold the pieces.

FARFALLE
The name means "bow ties." Those shown here are commercially made from flour-and-water pasta, but they can be hand-made from egg pasta, as on page 41.

CONCHIGLIE
These are "shells," available in many different sizes. The smallest are usually used in soups and the middle-sized ones for sauces. The largest are generally stuffed, although they are rare in Italy because the quantity of stuffing they require overwhelms the pasta.

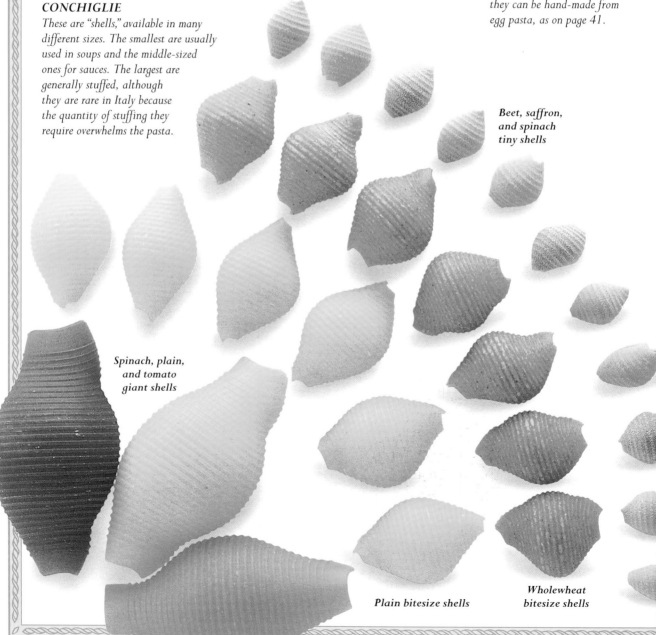

Beet, saffron, and spinach tiny shells

Spinach, plain, and tomato giant shells

Plain bitesize shells

Wholewheat bitesize shells

SAUCE SUGGESTIONS

You could try *lumache*, *gnocchi*, or *radiatori* with artichokes, *pancetta*, lemon juice, and thyme (*ai carciofi*, page 126). Or try *conchiglie*, *lumache*, or *gnocchi*, each of which can hold a meaty sauce, such as a *ragù* (pages 62 and 114).

Farfalle al salmone (page 121)

Conchiglie alla salsiccia e panna (page 125)

Orecchiette with broccoli (see Orecchiette alla verza, page 129)

GNOCCHI

The real gnocchi *are potato dumplings, and these pasta shapes are made to resemble them.* Gnocchetti *are small* gnocchi, *and* sardi *indicates Sardinian-style.*

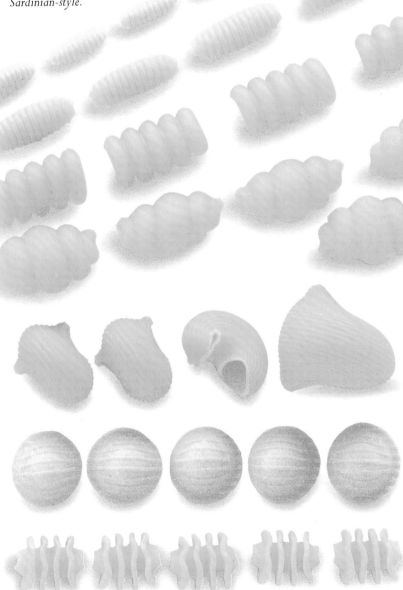

Gnocchetti sardi

Gnocchi sardi

Riccioli (or "curly"), also known as gnocchetti

Gnocchi

LUMACHE

Their name translates as "snails," a reference to their curled, snail-like shape. The larger one on the right is a lumacone, or "fat snail."

ORECCHIETTE

A speciality of Apulia, in southeastern Italy. The name means "little ears." They are traditionally made by hand from an eggless hardwheat pasta dough pressed between the thumb and palm.

RADIATORI

These shapes are called "radiators" because they resemble little heaters.

FORME SPECIALI

Special Shapes

FUSILLI

These shapes are also referred to as fusilli corti, *or "short springs," to differentiate them from the* fusilli *shown with the long pastas (page 15).* Eliche *means propeller, and these are a slightly looser spiral. The* fusilli bucati *have a hole running through them, as indicated by the word* bucati, *which means "bored."*

Plain, tomato, and spinach fusilli

Plain fusilli

Spinach fusilli

Wholewheat fusilli

Eliche

Fusilli bucati

SAUCE SUGGESTIONS

Fusilli are versatile and therefore prominent in the pasta-lover's diet. They lend themselves well to vegetable sauces: try *alle zucchine* (shown right), *alla campagnola* (page 122), *al cavolfiore* (page 120), or *alla verza* (page 129).

Fusilli corti alle zucchine (page 120)

Strozzapreti ai porcini e peperoni (page 128)

Ruote di carro con peperonata (page 124)

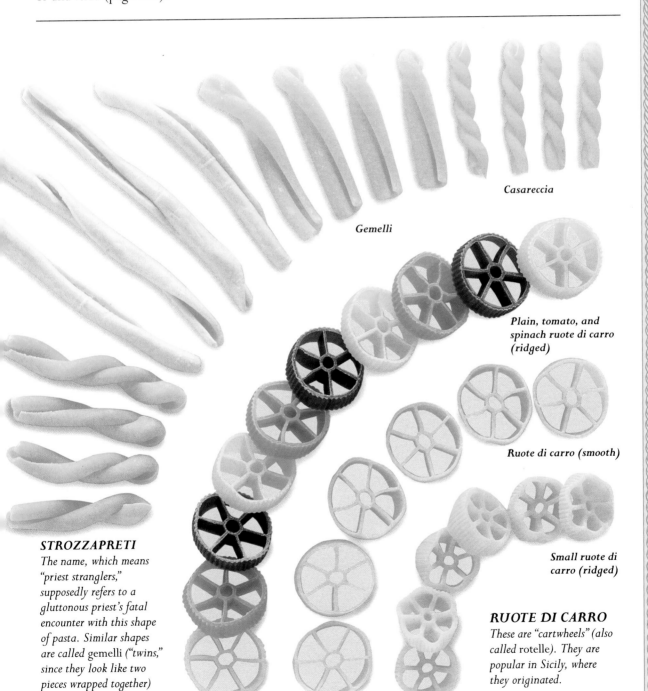

Casareccia

Gemelli

Plain, tomato, and spinach ruote di carro (ridged)

Ruote di carro (smooth)

Small ruote di carro (ridged)

STROZZAPRETI

The name, which means "priest stranglers," supposedly refers to a gluttonous priest's fatal encounter with this shape of pasta. Similar shapes are called gemelli *("twins," since they look like two pieces wrapped together) or* casareccia *("twists").*

RUOTE DI CARRO

These are "cartwheels" (also called rotelle*). They are popular in Sicily, where they originated.*

25

PASTA PER MINESTRE

Soup Pasta

The small shapes are collectively referred to as *pastina*, "little pasta," and the endings to their names, such as *ine* or *ini* and *etti* or *ette*, indicate "small." Except for *maltagliati* and occasionally *quadrucci*, they are reserved for homemade meat broth and given as a comforting meal to children or adults feeling under the weather. The shapes that resemble rice kernels, melon seeds, peppercorns, stars, and so on are created to amuse children or to look attractive rather than for differences in flavor or texture.

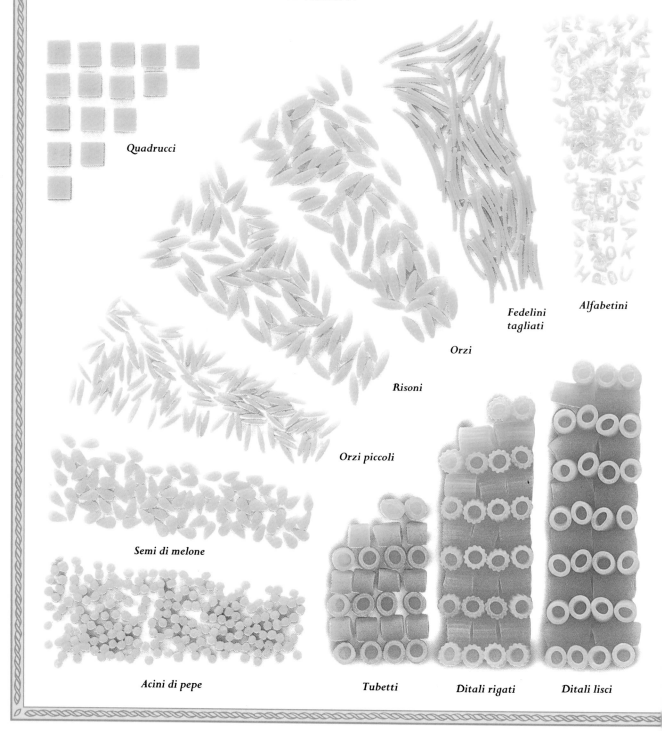

Quadrucci

Fedelini tagliati

Alfabetini

Orzi

Risoni

Orzi piccoli

Semi di melone

Acini di pepe

Tubetti

Ditali rigati

Ditali lisci

Soup Suggestions

Maltagliati is the classic choice for pasta and bean soup (*pasta e fagioli*), far right. *Stelline*, "little stars," are used to brighten up the children's soup, center.

Minestra di pasta e verdure alla romana (page 132)

Minestrina dei bambini (page 131)

Pasta e fagioli (page 131)

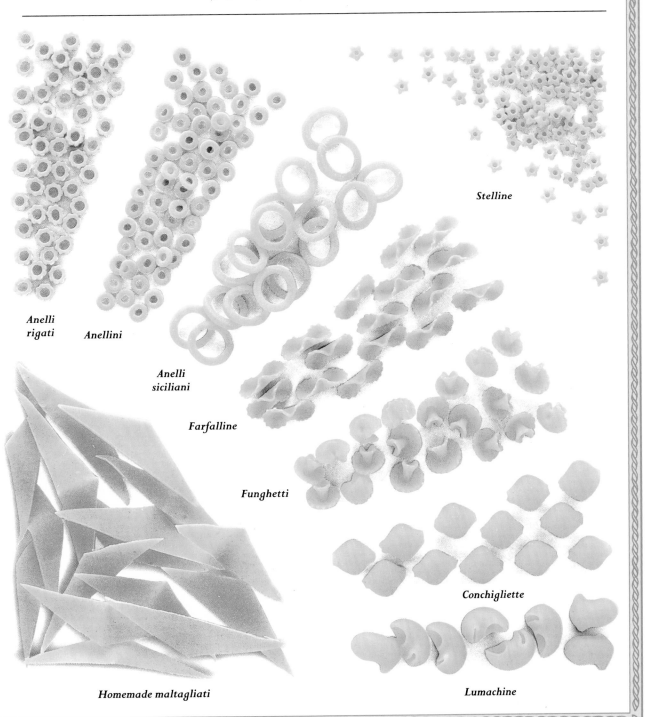

Anelli rigati

Anellini

Anelli siciliani

Farfalline

Funghetti

Stelline

Conchigliette

Homemade maltagliati

Lumachine

PASTA RIPIENA
Stuffed Pasta

Homemade stuffed pastas and layered pastas for baking make some of the most elegant and delicious pasta dishes. It is important that the quantity and kind of stuffing complement the shape of pasta. The most common mistake is to overpower the pasta – it should not be simply a receptacle for the stuffing but an integral part of the dish.

RAVIOLINI
Known as agnolotti *in Piedmont. They are usually filled with meat but also lend themselves to a variety of other stuffings.*

PANSOTI
Triangular pasta parcels, native to the Italian Riviera, whose name means "little bellies." They are filled with ricotta *and five local wild greens, and served with* walnut *pesto (see page 96).*

TORTELLONI
These square, stuffed pastas are usually filled with Swiss chard (or spinach) and ricotta. *They are served with butter and lots of* parmigiano-reggiano, *or with Burro e pomodoro sauce (see page 52). In Emilia they are called* tortelli.

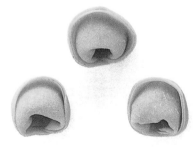

TORTELLINI
These are a speciality of Bologna and are served with broth on New Year's Eve or with cream sauce (see page 134).

CANNELLONI
Rectangular sheets of pasta, cannelloni *are thinly spread with one of a variety of fillings, rolled up to resemble a jelly roll and then baked.*

STUFFING SUGGESTIONS

Stuffings can be made from seafood, vegetables, or meat. Cheese of some kind is usually present and egg yolk is often used to bind together the ingredients.

Sweet potato, parsley, and mortadella (see Tortelli alla ferrarese, page 138)

Ricotta, ground beef, and mortadella (see Cannelloni di carne, page 144)

Spinach, ricotta, and prosciutto (see Tortelloni di biete, page 134)

CAPPELLETTI, TORTELLONI

Cappelletti *are "little hats," similar to* tortellini *but made from a square of pasta rather than a circle so that they form a peak. The larger ones are from Bologna and are called, confusingly,* tortelloni, *the same name as the flat, square parcels on the opposite page.*

Tortelloni

Cappelletti

LASAGNE

Large sheets of pasta, lasagne *are used to make up the dish with which their name has become synonymous. The pasta sheets are sandwiched together with thin layers of meat, seafood, or vegetable filling and then baked.*

Plain and spinach lasagne

PASTA COLORATA

Colored Pasta

Colored and flavored pasta is becoming increasingly popular outside Italy, but not within, where it is in conflict with the philosophy of Italian cooking whose ultimate concern is taste, rather than the appearance of food. A color would be of no gastronomic interest unless it contributed a desirable flavor. Only spinach and tomato pastas achieve this. Outside Italy, pasta-makers are experimenting with a range of colors and flavors, as illustrated here.

PLAIN

Plain egg pasta varies from pale to rich gold in color depending on the yolks used. Flour-and-water pasta has a warm yellow hue depending on the quality of the wheat.

TOMATO

Red pasta is traditionally made with dried tomato powder, but since this is rarely available commercially, a good substitute is double-concentrate tomato paste.

SPINACH

Green pasta can be made with fresh or frozen spinach, cooked and finely chopped, then added to the eggs before the flour is mixed in.

Saffron

Beet

Basil

Mushroom

Squid's ink

MAKING AND SERVING PASTA

Making pasta should be considered a craft, but it is one that anyone can learn and is well worth the effort. Egg pasta that is handmade from start to finish is the best. If you have a machine, use it for thinning the dough and for cutting certain widths of ribbon. Avoid machines where the ingredients are poured in at one end and a finished pasta shape is extruded from the other. They are not capable of the gradual process required to achieve the structure and texture of fine egg pasta.

PASTA-MAKING EQUIPMENT

These are all the tools you will need to make homemade egg pasta. Almost all are readily available in kitchen-supply shops or department stores. If you have difficulty finding a suitable rolling pin, try to have one custom-cut from a hardwood dowel at a lumber yard. You can get by without a pasta machine if you learn to roll and cut pasta by hand.

DOUGH SCRAPER
This is made of flexible metal or plastic and is used for scraping the sticky egg-and-flour mixture off the work surface before kneading.

COOKIE CUTTERS
Straight or fluted cookie cutters in various diameters are ideal for cutting circles of pasta for stuffing.

SMOOTH, WARM SURFACE
Traditionally pasta dough is made on a large wooden board. A laminated plastic surface, such as formica or laminex, also works well. Cold surfaces such as marble or metal are not suitable.

FORK
Use this to beat the eggs in the flour well and to draw in the flour until the mixture is thick enough to knead.

KITCHEN TOWEL
You need several clean and dry kitchen towels to absorb the moisture from freshly made pasta before it is cut, cooked or stored.

PLASTIC WRAP
When pasta dough is not being worked on, it must be wrapped tightly in plastic wrap to prevent it from drying and forming a crust on the surface.

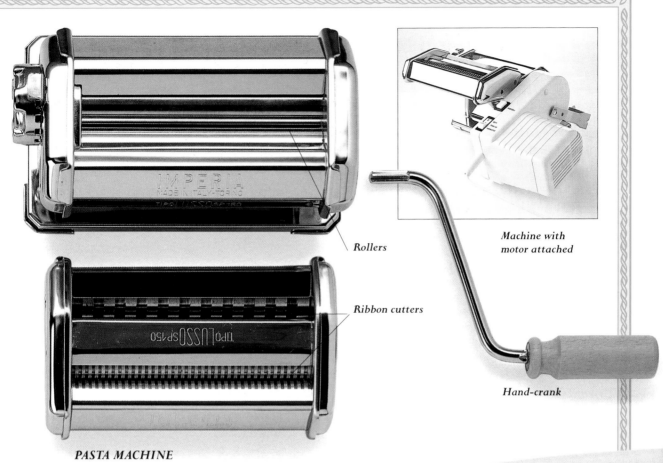

Rollers

Ribbon cutters

Machine with
motor attached

Hand-crank

PASTA MACHINE
The machine has rollers to thin out the pasta and
cutters to produce ribbons of various widths. You can
operate it with a hand-crank or an optional electric
motor. The motor is less tiring to use, frees both hands,
and enables you to produce more evenly rolled sheets.

PASTRY BAG
You can place fillings on a sheet of
pasta with a teaspoon, but a pastry
bag will make the job easier and faster.

ROLLING PIN
The traditional pasta rolling pin
used in Bologna is 1½in thick
and 32in long, with rounded,
smooth ends. However, a rolling
pin up to 2in thick and at least
24in long is fine for up to three
eggs' worth of dough.

PASTRY CUTTER
This rolling cutter is used for cutting
and sealing stuffed pasta and for
cutting ribbons with fluted edges.

GARGANELLI MAKER
The closest thing to an authentic Bolognese
garganelli tool is this wooden butter pat
used with a wooden dowel or round pencil
(see page 41).

KNIFE
Use a long chef's knife for cutting
pasta by hand, or the dough into
manageable chunks that can go
through the machine to be thinned.

MAKING THE DOUGH

Making pasta dough by hand is simple and with practice will easily become second nature. It also produces a far superior pasta than kneading by machine. The slower, more gradual process of hand-kneading, as well as the warmth from your hands, greatly enhances the elasticity and texture of the dough. The amount of flour given is approximate: it varies depending on the size of the eggs and the humidity of the environment. You can adjust before you begin to knead.

MIXING THE FLOUR AND EGGS

INGREDIENTS

3 large eggs
2¼ cups all-purpose flour (if possible use Italian "OO" flour)

1 Pour the flour into a mound on a wooden or other smooth, warm work surface and make a well in the center with your fingers.

2 Break the eggs one by one into the center of the well.

3 Beat the eggs gently with a fork until the yolks and whites are evenly mixed together.

4 With the fork, gradually incorporate the flour from the well into the eggs until the eggs are no longer runny. Do not break the wall of flour or the eggs will escape.

TIPS FOR MAKING THE DOUGH

- *Use eggs that are at room temperature.*

- *Do not knead the dough on a cold surface such as marble.*

COLORED PASTA

RED PASTA
For each egg, add 1 Tb of tomato paste. Mix it into the beaten eggs in the well before you start incorporating the flour.

GREEN PASTA
For each egg, use 4oz of fresh spinach or 2½oz of thawed frozen spinach. Cook in salted water (salt enhances the color), squeeze out excess water, and finely chop before using.

KNEADING THE DOUGH

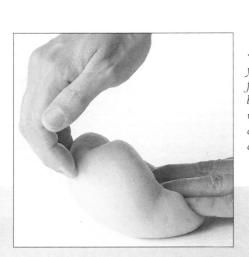

1 This step must be done quickly and without hesitation or you may end up losing some of the egg mixture. Using both hands, swiftly bring the remaining flour over the egg mixture so that it is completely covered.

2 Begin working the mass with your hands until all the flour is mixed in with the eggs. Decide whether you need more flour: the dough should feel moist but not sticky. When it is the right consistency, wrap it tightly in plastic wrap.

3 Scrape away any dough stuck to the work surface, and wash your hands to remove any egg and flour. Unwrap the dough and begin kneading. Hold the dough with one hand while folding it over with the fingers of the other hand.

4 Use the heel of your palm to push the dough down and away from you. Rotate the dough a quarter turn and repeat the two-part process. Continue until the dough is uniform and very smooth. Immediately wrap it in plastic wrap and let it rest for at least 20 minutes before rolling it out.

ROLLING THE PASTA

Rolling by hand produces a more desirable pasta than rolling by machine. When you roll by hand the dough is stretched rather than compressed. This creates a more porous pasta that absorbs sauce better as well as having a more interesting texture. Practice a couple of times on dough that you are happy to discard until you feel you have it right. If you do use a machine, get the optional motor attachment so that your hands are free to feed in the dough.

ROLLING BY HAND

Be prepared to throw away your first few hand-rolled sheets – you are unlikely to get the hang of rolling pasta in one try. First remove the dough from the plastic wrap. Knead it again for about a minute so that the moisture that has collected on the surface is worked back into the dough. Flatten the dough a little with your hands to form a round disk and place it on the work surface.

1 *Begin rolling from two-thirds of the way down the disk and stop just before the top edge. Stop, turn the disk 90°, and repeat. Continue until the dough is ¼ in thick.*

2 *Roll the top edge of the dough on to the pin. Hold the dough at the bottom while you gently stretch and roll it on to the pin. Turn the dough on the pin 90°, unroll and repeat five times.*

3 *Roll the dough snugly back onto the pin from the top. As you roll the pin back and forth, slide your hands together and apart to trace the shape of a W. When the dough is rolled up, turn it with the pin, unroll and repeat.*

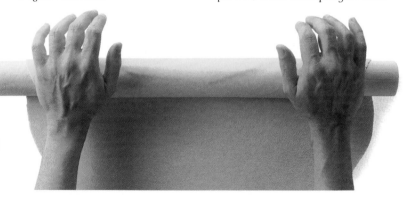

4 *Continue stretching the dough until it is transparent, letting it drape over the edge of the worktop. Lay the dough on a kitchen towel to dry.*

TIPS FOR HAND-ROLLING

• *Have only the palms of your hands in contact with the dough on the rolling pin.*

• *To stretch rather than compress the dough, do not push down on it but out and away from you.*

ROLLING BY MACHINE

Roll the dough through the machine one notch at a time. Trying to speed the thinning process by skipping notches on the rollers will result in pasta of a poor texture. Pasta needs to be thinned out gradually to give it elasticity.

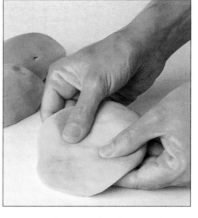

1 Cut a three-egg dough into at least six pieces. Flatten one with your hand and wrap the rest in plastic wrap.

2 With the rollers at their widest setting, feed the dough into the machine. Pick up the dough as it comes through but don't stretch or pull it.

3 Fold the dough in thirds, turn it so the folds are at the sides, and run it through the machine again. Do this three or four times until the dough is very smooth. Repeat with the other pieces.

4 Reduce the width of the rollers by one notch. Run all the pieces through the machine once, laying them out on dry kitchen towels. Reduce the width by one notch again, and repeat. Continue until all the pieces have gone through the machine at each setting down to the thinnest.

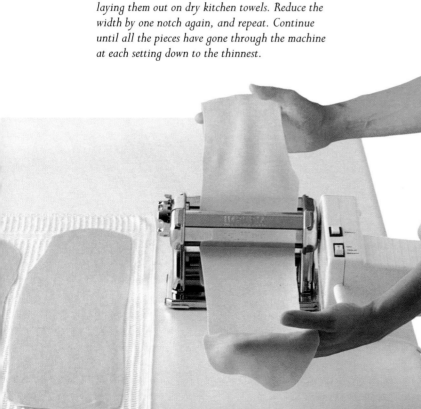

CUTTING THE PASTA

Before you cut pasta it must dry until it feels leathery so that the noodles will not stick to each other, but not dry so much that it becomes too brittle to cut. If you use a pasta machine to roll out the dough, the pieces will be just the right size and shape to feed back through the machine's cutting attachment to make *fettuccine* and *tonnarelli*. Other shapes need to be cut by hand, which is simple and requires only a little practice. Hand-rolled pasta must, of course, be hand-cut.

CUTTING BY HAND

FETTUCCINE (⅕in) AND *TAGLIATELLE (⅓in)*

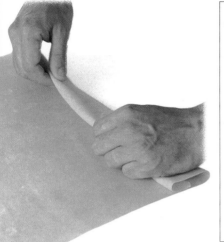  

1 Loosely roll up the sheet of pasta dough into a flat roll about 2in across.

2 Take a large knife, rest the flat of the blade against your knuckles, and cut the roll of pasta into ribbons of the desired width by moving your knuckles back along the roll after every cut.

3 Unravel the ribbons. To store them (dried pasta keeps for months), wrap loosely around your hand into nests and put on a kitchen towel to dry. To use the same day, lay them flat.

CAPELLI D'ANGELO
To make angel hair, follow the procedure above but cut the pasta as thinly as possible.

MALTAGLIATI
Make two diagonal cuts followed by a straight cut perpendicular to the roll of pasta. Separate the little piles.

QUADRUCCI
Cut the pasta as for tagliatelle, *above*, then, without unravelling, cut the ribbons crosswise into small squares.

PAPPARDELLE
To make the saw-edged version, use a fluted pastry cutter on flat sheets of pasta. For straight-edged, roll up the pasta and cut ribbons ¾ in wide.

FARFALLE
Cut a sheet of pasta into 1½ in squares using a fluted pastry cutter. Pinch the squares in the middle, with one fold on top and two on the bottom.

GARGANELLI
Roll 1½ in pasta squares on to a pencil over the teeth of a comb or butter pat. Press down on the pencil edges, not the pasta itself, and the garganelli will slide off easily.

CUTTING BY MACHINE

FETTUCCINE
Roll the pasta to the thinnest setting of the rollers. Use a knife to cut the pasta into strips about 1 foot long. Attach the cutters to the machine and pass the strips of pasta through the wider set. Store machine-cut pasta the same way as hand-cut pasta.

TONNARELLI
Thin the pasta to the penultimate setting of the rollers, then pass the sheets through the narrower cutters of the machine attachment. Because the pasta sheet is thick, and the cutting measure narrow, the resulting ribbon is square in cross-section.

STUFFING THE PASTA

Except for *tortellini* and *cappelletti*, which require a little bit of practice, all the other stuffed pasta shapes are easy to make and require no special skill. Your biggest enemy in making stuffed pastas will be pasta that is too dry to work with.

To help avoid that problem, always keep the dough you are not working on tightly wrapped in plastic wrap until you are ready to use it. You could also add about 2 teaspoons of milk to a two-egg batch of dough when you mix the eggs.

TORTELLONI

1 Tortelloni *in Romagna, tortelli in Emilia are squares of pasta with filling in the middle. Take a strip of pasta 4in wide and place stuffing on it at 2in intervals. You need the equivalent of a rounded teaspoon of stuffing.*

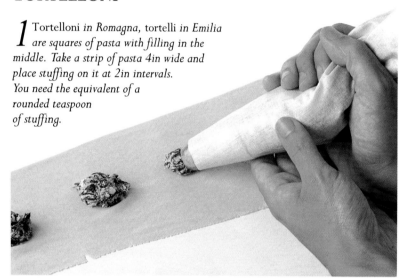

2 Moisten the edges of the pasta and fold it over. Cut between the stuffing (at 2in intervals) and along the bottom edge with a fluted cutter. Pinch the edges together to seal.

TORTELLINI

2 Fold the disk in half, then pull the two corners together, wrapping them around the tip of your finger. Pinch the ends together.

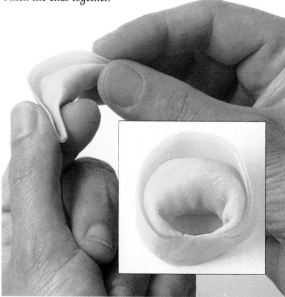

1 Cut 2in disks from a thin sheet of pasta using a plain cookie cutter. Place about ½ teaspoon of stuffing in the center of each disk.

TORTELLONI FROM BOLOGNA

1 For Bolognese tortelloni, *cut a thin sheet of pasta into 3in squares and place about a rounded teaspoon of stuffing in the center of each one.*

2 *Moisten the edges with a wet finger and fold each square in half to form a triangle. Pinch the edges together to seal.*

3 *Pull two corners together, wrapping them around the tip of your finger and indenting the parcel where filled with stuffing. Pinch the corners together where they join.*

RAVIOLINI

1 *Cut 2in disks from a thin sheet of pasta using a fluted cookie cutter.*

2 *Place about ½ teaspoon of stuffing in the center of each disk.*

3 *Fold each disk in half, pinching the edges with your fingers to seal them. Gently pull down the two corners to form a crescent.*

VARIATIONS

PANSOTI
Place stuffing in the center of 2in squares of pasta and fold in half.

RAVIOLINI
For smooth-edged raviolini, use a plain cookie cutter or a glass.

CAPPELLETTI
These are like tortellini but made from a square. They resemble bishop's mitres.

43

COOKING AND SERVING

Cooking pasta is easy and just takes a little practice and intuition. Ignore the directions on dried, store-bought pasta: the only way of knowing when it is done is to taste it. It should be firm to the bite but chewable. Remember, it will continue to cook as you drain and toss it. Cooking time will vary with the shape and brand. Homemade pasta cooks very quickly. If newly made, it cooks in less than a minute. For stuffed pastas, taste the edge where the parcel is sealed.

BOILING THE PASTA

1 Use a large saucepan or pot so that there is room for the pasta to move around in the water. Bring the water to the boil before adding salt or pasta. Add all the pasta at once.

2 Stir the pasta right away to prevent it from sticking to the pot or to itself, and also to submerge long strands. Never break long pasta to fit it into the pot. Cover the pot until the water resumes boiling.

3 Stir periodically and taste to see if the pasta is al dente, or firm to the bite. At this point, it is done.

4 Drain the pasta in a colander immediately. Shake to dislodge excess water. Never rinse the pasta – this chills it and removes the coat of starch that helps the sauce cling to the pasta.

PASTA-TO-WATER

½lb pasta
3 quarts water

1lb pasta
4 quarts water

1½lbs pasta
5 quarts water

2lbs pasta
Use two pots

SALT

1 Tb salt for
4 quarts water

SERVING

1 Transfer the pasta to a warmed serving bowl and add the sauce. Alternatively, add the pasta to the pan containing the sauce.

2 Toss with a fork and a spoon until the pasta is thoroughly coated with the sauce. Avoid the common mistake of serving a heap of pasta with the sauce simply placed on top of it.

TWIRLING

To twirl long pasta onto a fork, pick up a few strands, lifting them away from the others. With the tip of the fork prongs against the side of the plate, rotate the fork until the strands are completely rolled onto it. The knack is to pick up only a few strands at the outset or you will end up with an unmanageable ball of pasta on your fork.

CLASSIC SAUCES

The pasta sauces here are some of the more popular traditional ones. A definitive recipe does not exist for any of them; instead there are many versions, all of which are equally authentic. Mine are based on personal preference, and on the way I have eaten them and seen them being made as I was growing up.

Each recipe serves 6 people if followed by a second course, or 4 people if served on its own

SPAGHETTINI
AGLIO E OLIO
Spaghettini with Garlic and Olive Oil

This dish has been my savior during many a late-night hunger attack. It is quick and easy and, with good quality pasta and olive oil, immensely satisfying. Take the sauce off the heat as soon as it is ready, even if the pasta is not yet done. The oil will hold its heat for the extra minutes you need to finish off the pasta, and you will avoid the risk of burning the garlic.

INGREDIENTS

For 1lb dried, store-bought pasta

½ cup extra-virgin olive oil
1 tsp finely chopped garlic
1 Tb finely chopped flat-leaf parsley
¼ tsp red pepper flakes
salt

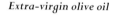

Extra-virgin olive oil

PREPARATION

1 Bring 4 quarts of water to a boil in a large saucepan or pot. Add 1 tablespoon of salt and the pasta, stirring until the strands are submerged.
2 Put the olive oil and the garlic in a large skillet over a medium-high heat. When the garlic begins to change color, add the parsley, red pepper flakes and some salt. Stir well and remove from the heat.
3 When the pasta is cooked *al dente*, return the skillet with the sauce to a low heat, drain the pasta, and add it to the skillet. Toss until the pasta is well coated with the sauce, correct for salt and spiciness, and serve at once.

PASTA CHOICE

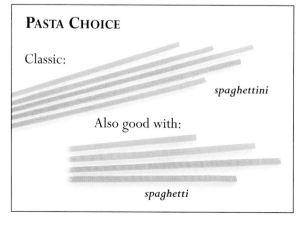

Classic:

spaghettini

Also good with:

spaghetti

Garlic

Flat-leaf parsley

Red pepper
flakes

Salt

Spaghettini
aglio e olio

PESTO DI BASILICO
ALLA GENOVESE
Genoese Basil Pesto

The only way to have true Genoese *pesto* is to go to the Liguria region of Italy where the tiny fragrant sweet basil for which the Italian Riviera is famous can be found. Locally grown basil, although not quite the same, will produce a perfectly acceptable alternative for those of us who may find it impractical to fly to the Riviera whenever we feel like having *pesto*.

INGREDIENTS

For pasta made with 3 eggs (see page 36)
***or* 1lb dried, store-bought pasta**

2oz fresh basil leaves
½ cup extra-virgin olive oil
2 Tbs pine nuts
2 cloves garlic, peeled
salt
½ cup freshly grated parmigiano-reggiano *cheese*
2 Tbs freshly grated pecorino romano *cheese*
3 Tbs butter, softened to room temperature

**Extra-virgin
olive oil**

PREPARATION

1 Put the basil leaves, olive oil, pine nuts, garlic, and 1 teaspoon of salt into a food processor or blender and grind until fine and almost creamy.

You can prepare the sauce ahead of time up to this point and refrigerate or even freeze it. Cover the surface with olive oil to prevent the basil turning black.

2 Transfer the mixture to a large bowl and stir in the two grated cheeses.
3 Bring 4 quarts of water to a boil in a large saucepan or pot. Add 1 tablespoon of salt and the pasta, stir well and cook until *al dente*. Drain and toss with the sauce, 2 tablespoons of hot water, and the butter.

Basil

PASTA CHOICE
Good with:

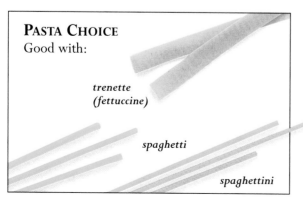

*trenette
(fettuccine)*

spaghetti

spaghettini

Garlic

Salt

Parmigiano-reggiano

Pecorino romano

Butter

Pine nuts

Trenette with pesto di basilico

SUGO AL
BURRO E POMODORO

Butter and Tomato Sauce

This is probably the simplest of all pasta sauces and will evoke childhood memories for many an Italian. If you want a pure tomato sauce, it has no equal. Use fresh tomatoes if you can, although canned are better than poor-quality fresh ones.

INGREDIENTS

For pasta made with 3 eggs (see page 36)
or **1lb dried, store-bought pasta**

2lbs fresh ripe plum tomatoes, peeled, seeded and coarsely chopped, or 3 cups canned whole peeled tomatoes, with their juice, coarsely chopped
6 Tbs butter
1 medium-sized onion, peeled and cut in half
salt
4 Tbs freshly grated parmigiano-reggiano *cheese*

PREPARATION

1 Put all the ingredients except the cheese in a saucepan and simmer over a low heat until the tomatoes have reduced and separated from the butter: 20–40 minutes depending on the size of the pan. Remove from the heat and set aside, discarding the onion halves.

You can prepare the sauce ahead of time and refrigerate (it keeps for 3–4 days in the refrigerator in a tightly lidded jar) or freeze it.

2 Bring 4 quarts of water to a boil in a large saucepan or pot. Add 1 tablespoon of salt and the pasta, stir well, and cook the pasta until *al dente*. Drain and toss with the sauce and grated cheese.

Fresh plum tomatoes

Butter

Onion

PEELING AND SEEDING A TOMATO

1 *Peel the tomato using a swivel-bladed peeler. Use a side-to-side, sawing motion at the same time as you peel downwards.*

2 *Halve the tomato, then scoop out the seeds with your thumb and discard them. You can then coarsely chop the tomato flesh.*

Tortelloni di spinaci
with sugo al burro
e pomodoro

Salt

Parmigiano-reggiano

PASTA CHOICE
Good with:

bucatini

penne lisce

tortelloni
di spinaci

spaghetti

SPAGHETTINI AL
POMODORO E BASILICO

Spaghettini with Tomatoes, Basil, Olive Oil, and Garlic

This is a quick and easy summery sauce, one I can eat often without tiring of it, and ideal when fresh, ripe tomatoes are abundant. The red pepper flakes, if you choose to use them, are not intended to make the sauce spicy but simply to give it a little liveliness, so be gentle with the pinch. While the amount of garlic may seem overgenerous, it is less pungent when sliced and stewed than when chopped and browned. You get a sweeter flavor from fresh tomatoes than from canned.

INGREDIENTS

For 1lb dried, store-bought pasta

¼ cup extra-virgin olive oil
3 Tbs thinly sliced garlic
2lbs fresh ripe plum tomatoes, peeled, seeded and thinly
sliced lengthwise, *or* 3 cups canned whole peeled
tomatoes, with their juice, coarsely chopped
salt
¼ cup fresh basil leaves, torn by hand
into ½ in pieces
pinch of red pepper flakes (optional)

PREPARATION

1 Put all but 1 tablespoon of the olive oil and all the garlic in a large skillet over a medium-high heat and cook until the garlic begins to sizzle.
2 Add the tomatoes as soon as the garlic begins to change color. If using fresh tomatoes, you'll notice they give off a fair amount of liquid. When the liquid begins to reduce, season with salt. If using canned tomatoes, season with salt at the beginning. Continue cooking over a medium-high heat until the tomatoes have reduced and separated from the oil: 10–20 minutes depending on the size of the skillet.
3 While the sauce is cooking, bring 4 quarts of water to a boil in a large saucepan or pot.
4 When the sauce has reduced, add the torn basil leaves and the optional pinch of red pepper flakes. Cook for 1–2 minutes, then remove from the heat and set aside.
5 Add 1 tablespoon of salt to the boiling water in the saucepan. Drop in the pasta, stirring until the strands are submerged. When cooked *al dente*, drain and toss with the sauce in the skillet, adding the remaining tablespoon of olive oil. Taste for salt and serve at once.

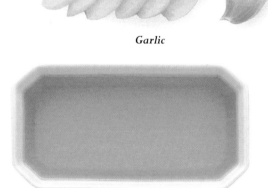

Garlic

Extra-virgin olive oil

PASTA CHOICE
Classic:

spaghettini

Also good with:

spaghetti

*penne
lisce*

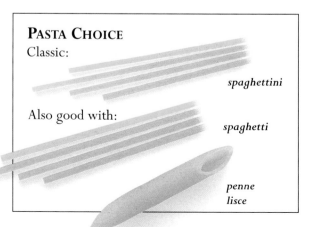

Fresh plum
tomatoes

Salt

Basil

Red pepper
flakes

**Spaghettini
al pomodoro
e basilico**

PENNE
ALL'ARRABBIATA
Penne with Spicy Tomato Sauce

The name of this pasta means it is "angry" because it is hot and spicy, and it is popular in Rome and central Italy. Increase or decrease the amount of red pepper flakes according to the intensity of "anger" you desire.

INGREDIENTS

For 1lb dried, store-bought pasta

⅓ cup plus 1 Tb extra-virgin olive oil
½ tsp finely chopped garlic
2oz pancetta, cut from a ¼in thick slice
into thin strips
3 cups canned whole peeled tomatoes,
with their juice, coarsely chopped
¼ tsp red pepper flakes
salt
12 medium-sized fresh basil leaves, torn by hand
into ½in pieces
2 Tbs freshly grated pecorino romano cheese

PREPARATION

1 Put all but 1 tablespoon of the olive oil and all the garlic in a large skillet over a medium-high heat and cook until the garlic begins to sizzle.
2 Add the *pancetta* strips and cook until the *pancetta* is well browned but not crisp.
3 Add the canned tomatoes, the red pepper flakes and a little salt (note that the *pancetta* is already salty). Reduce the heat and simmer until the tomatoes have reduced and separated from the oil: 30–40 minutes depending on the size of the skillet. Remove from the heat and set aside.

 You can prepare the sauce ahead of time up to this point and refrigerate it.

4 Bring 4 quarts of water to a boil in a large saucepan or pot, add 1 tablespoon of salt and the pasta, stirring well.
5 Return the skillet with the sauce to a medium heat and add the torn basil leaves. When the pasta is cooked *al dente*, drain, and toss with the sauce in the skillet, turning off the heat. Stir in the remaining tablespoon of olive oil and the grated cheese. Taste for spiciness and serve at once.

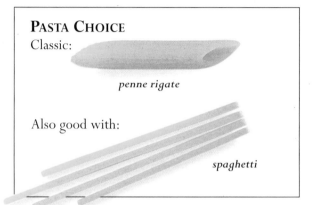

PASTA CHOICE
Classic:

penne rigate

Also good with:

spaghetti

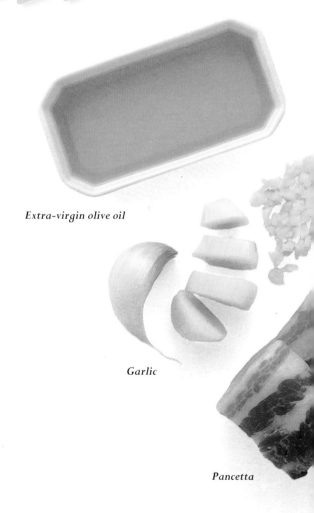

Extra-virgin olive oil

Garlic

Pancetta

Penne
all'arrabbiata

Pecorino
romano

Canned
tomatoes

Red pepper
flakes

Salt

Basil

57

SPAGHETTI ALLA
PUTTANESCA

Spaghetti with Tomatoes, Capers, Olives, and Anchovies

Puttana means prostitute and this is the pasta dish she would use to seduce her clients. While I cannot guarantee its success as an aphrodisiac, I can at least guarantee that your partner will enjoy the food!

Extra-virgin olive oil

INGREDIENTS

For 1lb dried, store-bought pasta

⅓ cup plus 1 Tb extra-virgin olive oil
6 anchovy fillets, chopped
½ tsp finely chopped garlic
3 cups canned whole peeled tomatoes,
with their juice, coarsely chopped
salt
2 tsps coarsely chopped fresh oregano *or* ½ tsp dried
2 Tbs capers
8 – 10 black olives, pitted and julienned

Anchovies

Garlic

PREPARATION

1 Put all but 1 tablespoon of the olive oil and all the anchovies in a large skillet over a low heat and cook, stirring with a wooden spoon, until the anchovies dissolve.
2 Add the garlic and cook for about 15 seconds, taking care not to brown it.
3 Raise the heat to medium-high and add the tomatoes with a pinch of salt. When the sauce comes to a boil, turn the heat down and simmer until the tomatoes have reduced and separated from the oil: 20 – 40 minutes depending on the size of the skillet. Remove from the heat and set aside.

You can prepare the sauce ahead of time up to this point and refrigerate it.

4 Bring 4 quarts of water to a boil in a large saucepan or pot, add 1 tablespoon of salt and the pasta, stirring until the strands are submerged.
5 When the pasta is halfway done, return the skillet with the sauce to a medium heat, adding the oregano, capers and olives.
6 When the pasta is cooked *al dente*, drain and toss with the sauce in the skillet over a low heat, adding the remaining tablespoon of olive oil. Taste for salt and serve at once.

Canned tomatoes

Spaghetti alla
puttanesca

Salt

Fresh oregano

Capers

Olives

PASTA CHOICE

Classic:

Also good with:

spaghettini

spaghetti

penne lisce

FETTUCCINE
PRIMAVERA
Fettuccine with Spring Vegetables and Cream

Outside Italy this recipe is widely popular but often prepared incorrectly. The most frequent mistake is to fail to sauté the vegetables for long enough to concentrate their flavor. Done properly, this is a perfectly balanced, heavenly dish.

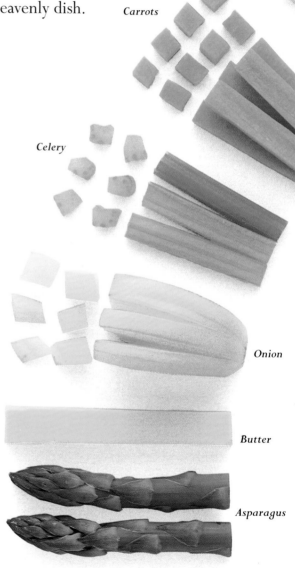

Carrots

Celery

Onion

Butter

Asparagus

INGREDIENTS

For pasta made with 3 eggs (see page 36)
or **1lb dried, store-bought pasta**

4oz asparagus
4 Tbs butter
¼ cup finely chopped yellow onion
¼ cup finely chopped celery
½ cup finely diced carrots
¾ cup finely diced zucchini
½ cup finely diced red bell pepper
salt and freshly ground black pepper
1 cup heavy cream
¼ cup freshly grated parmigiano-reggiano *cheese*
2 Tbs finely chopped flat-leaf parsley

PREPARATION

1 Trim and peel the lower green portions of the asparagus. Cook whole in salted boiling water in a skillet until tender. Cut into ¾in lengths.

2 Melt the butter in a large skillet over a medium-high heat. Add the onion and sauté to a rich golden color. Add the celery and carrot and sauté for another 5 minutes.

3 Add the zucchini and red bell pepper to the skillet and continue to sauté over a medium-high heat until all the vegetables are tender and lightly colored (approximately 10 – 20 minutes, depending on the size of the skillet). Add salt and black pepper to taste.

4 Add the asparagus to the skillet and sauté for about 1 minute. Add the cream and cook, stirring occasionally, until the cream has reduced by half, then remove from the heat and set aside.

5 While the cream is cooking, bring 4 quarts of water to a boil in a large saucepan or pot. Add 1 tablespoon of salt and the pasta to the boiling water in the saucepan, stirring.

6 When the pasta is cooked *al dente*, return the skillet with the sauce to a medium heat, drain the pasta and toss it with the sauce, adding the grated cheese and parsley. Serve at once.

PASTA CHOICE
Classic:

fettuccine

Also good with:

tagliatelle

Zucchini

Red bell
pepper

Salt

Black
pepper

Heavy cream

Parmigiano-
reggiano

Flat-leaf parsley

**Fettuccine
primavera**

TAGLIATELLE AL
RAGU
Tagliatelle with Meat Bolognese Sauce

As a child, my mouth would water in anticipation of those glorious moments when we would sit at the table and a steaming platter of *tagliatelle al ragù* with its irresistible aroma would arrive. The dish is a staple in Emilia-Romagna, the region where my family comes from, and is almost synonymous with its capital city, Bologna. This is the way my mother makes it, and the way my grandmother made it …

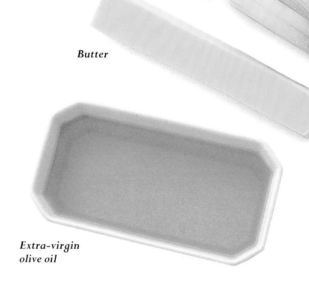

Onion

Butter

Extra-virgin olive oil

INGREDIENTS

For pasta made with 3 eggs (see page 36)
or **1lb dried, store-bought pasta**

3 Tbs extra-virgin olive oil
5 Tbs butter
2 Tbs finely chopped yellow onion
2 Tbs finely diced carrot
2 Tbs finely diced celery
¾ lb coarsely ground lean beef
salt
1 cup dry white wine
½ cup whole milk
⅛ tsp freshly grated nutmeg
2 cups canned whole peeled tomatoes,
with their juice, coarsely chopped
½ cup freshly grated parmigiano-reggiano cheese

PREPARATION

1 Put the olive oil, 3 tablespoons of the butter and all the onion in a heavy, deep saucepan over a medium-high heat and sauté until the onion has turned a light golden color.
2 Add the carrot and celery and continue sautéing until they begin to change color.
3 Add the beef, breaking it up with a wooden spoon. Add some salt and cook, stirring occasionally, until the meat is just browned.
4 Add the wine and cook, stirring occasionally, until it has completely evaporated. Add the milk and the nutmeg and continue to cook, stirring, until most of the milk has evaporated.
5 Add the tomatoes, stir, and once they start to bubble, turn the heat down to very low. Simmer uncovered for at least 3 hours, stirring occasionally.

You can prepare the sauce ahead of time up to this point and refrigerate or even freeze it. When reheating it, add a couple of tablespoons of water.

6 Bring 4 quarts of water to a boil in a large saucepan or pot. Add 1 tablespoon of salt and the pasta, stir well, and cook until *al dente*. Drain and toss with the hot or reheated sauce, the remaining butter and the freshly grated cheese. Taste for salt and serve at once.

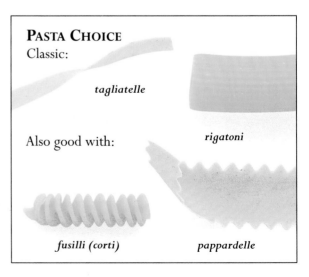

PASTA CHOICE
Classic:

tagliatelle

rigatoni

Also good with:

fusilli (corti)

pappardelle

RAGU

Carrot

Celery

Ground
beef

Salt

White wine

Milk

Nutmeg

Canned
tomatoes

Parmigiano-
reggiano

**Tagliatelle
al ragù**

FETTUCCINE
ALL'ALFREDO

Fettuccine with Butter and Cream

This is commonly thought of as a northern Italian dish but it actually comes from Rome. It is named after a restaurant owner, Alfredo, whose trademark was to give his pasta a final toss with a gold fork and spoon before sending it to the table.

INGREDIENTS

For pasta made with 3 eggs (see page 36)
***or* 1lb dried, store-bought pasta**

3 Tbs butter
1 cup heavy cream
pinch of freshly ground nutmeg
salt and freshly ground black pepper
½ cup freshly grated parmigiano-reggiano *cheese*

PREPARATION

1 Bring 4 quarts of water to a boil in a large saucepan or pot.
2 Put the butter and cream in a large skillet over a medium-high heat and boil, stirring frequently, until the cream has reduced almost by half. Add the freshly grated nutmeg, some salt and a generous amount of fresh black pepper. Remove from the heat and set aside.
3 Add 1 tablespoon of salt and the pasta to the boiling water in the saucepan, stirring well. When the pasta is cooked *al dente*, drain it and add it to the sauce in the skillet.
4 Add the freshly grated cheese to the skillet, then toss until the pasta is well coated with the sauce, and season with salt and pepper. Serve immediately.

Butter

Heavy cream

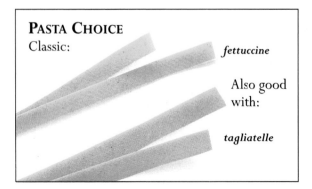

PASTA CHOICE
Classic:

fettuccine

Also good with:

tagliatelle

Fettuccine all'Alfredo

Parmigiano-reggiano

Nutmeg

Salt

Black pepper

SPAGHETTI ALLA
CARBONARA
Spaghetti with Pancetta and Raw Eggs

Many recipes I've seen for this dish call for cream. The way I learned to make it from my mother is without cream and this is still the way I prefer it – I find the creaminess from the eggs and cheese in contact with the hot pasta is enough. But I deviate from my mother's recipe in using just the yolk rather than the whole egg, which makes the dish a little richer. If *pancetta* is unavailable you can substitute good quality, lean bacon. It should be unsmoked.

INGREDIENTS

For 1lb dried, store-bought pasta

2 Tbs butter
2 Tbs extra-virgin olive oil
4oz pancetta, *cut from a ¼in thick slice
into thin strips*
⅓ cup dry white wine
4 egg yolks
3 Tbs freshly grated parmigiano-reggiano *cheese*
1 Tb freshly grated pecorino romano *cheese*
1 Tb finely chopped flat-leaf parsley
salt and freshly ground black pepper

PREPARATION

1 Bring 4 quarts of water to a boil in a large saucepan or pot.
2 Meanwhile, put the butter and olive oil in a small skillet over a medium-high heat. When the butter has melted, add the *pancetta* and cook until it is well browned but not crisp. Add the white wine and continue cooking until it has reduced by about half. Remove from the heat and set aside.
3 Add 1 tablespoon of salt and the pasta to the boiling water in the saucepan, stirring until the strands are submerged.
4 In a mixing bowl (large enough to hold the pasta), lightly beat the egg yolks with the two grated cheeses, the parsley, a pinch of salt and a generous amount of fresh black pepper.
5 When the pasta is cooked *al dente*, return the skillet with the *pancetta* to a high heat, then drain the pasta and add it to the mixing bowl containing the egg yolks and cheese. Toss until the pasta is well coated with the egg and cheese mixture, then add the hot *pancetta*. Toss again, then serve at once.

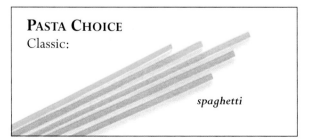

*White
wine*

Pancetta

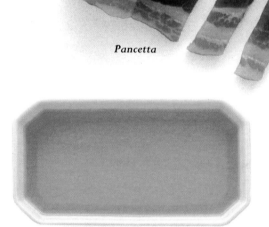

Extra-virgin olive oil

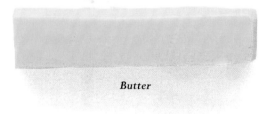

Butter

PASTA CHOICE
Classic:

spaghetti

Parmigiano-reggiano

Pecorino romano

Flat-leaf parsley

Salt

Black pepper

Egg yolks

Spaghetti alla carbonara

SPAGHETTI ALLE
VONGOLE

Spaghetti with Clams

The trick to getting the best flavor in this dish is to finish cooking the *spaghetti* in the pan along with the sauce so the pasta absorbs the juices that the clams gave off as they steamed open. The clams that take the longest to steam open in the pan are the freshest – don't discard them. Do, however, discard clams that are open when you buy them and don't snap shut if you tap them; they are dead.

Red pepper flakes

Flat-leaf parsley

Garlic

Extra-virgin olive oil

INGREDIENTS

For 1lb dried, store-bought pasta

⅓ cup extra-virgin olive oil
1 tsp finely chopped garlic
1 Tb finely chopped flat-leaf parsley
small pinch of red pepper flakes
48 baby clams in their shells, soaked
for 5 minutes, rinsed and scrubbed
under running water
salt
⅓ cup dry white wine
2 Tbs butter

PREPARATION

1 Put the olive oil and garlic in a large skillet (large enough to hold the clams and the pasta later) over a medium-high heat and cook until the garlic begins to sizzle. Stir in the parsley and the red pepper flakes.

2 Add the clams in their shells, season with salt and stir well. Add the wine and cook, stirring occasionally, until the alcohol evaporates: about 1 minute. Once the wine has evaporated, cover the skillet to steam the clams open.

3 While the clams are steaming, bring 4 quarts of water to a boil in a large saucepan or pot.

4 Check the clams frequently, and when they have all opened, remove the skillet from the heat.

5 Add 1 tablespoon of salt to the boiling water. Drop in the pasta and stir until the strands are submerged. When the pasta is *molto al dente* (about 1 minute away from being *al dente*), drain well.

6 Immediately, return the skillet with the clams to a medium heat and add the drained pasta so that it finishes cooking in the skillet. Cook until the pasta is *al dente* and most of the liquid in the skillet has evaporated. Stir in the butter and serve at once.

PASTA CHOICE
Classic:

spaghetti

Clams

Salt

White wine

Butter

Spaghetti alle vongole

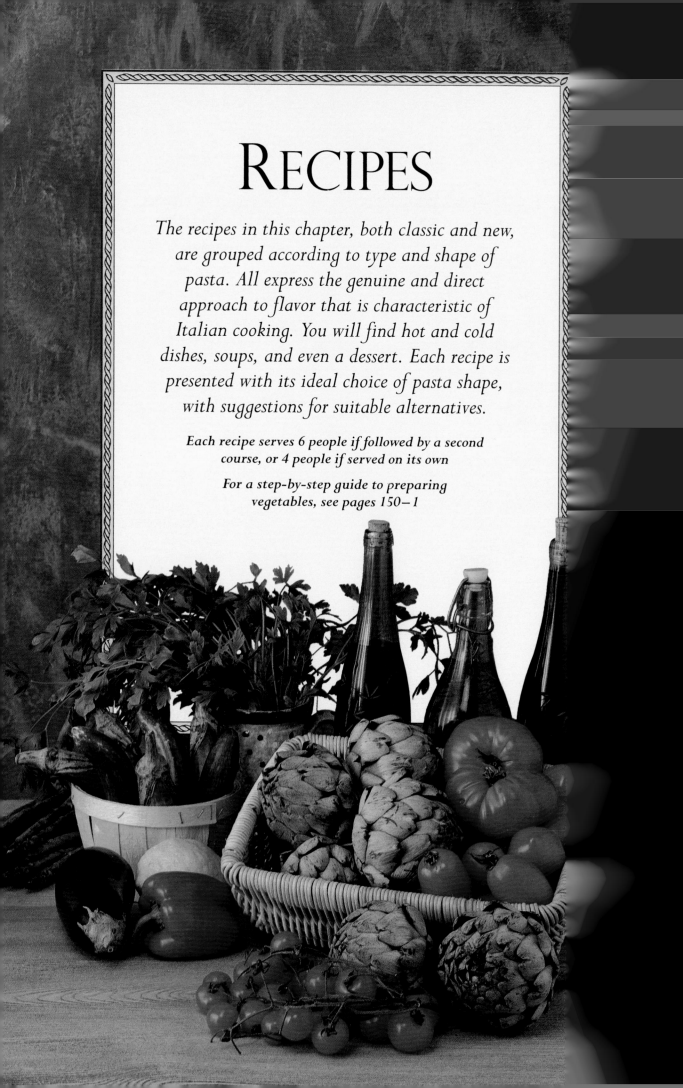

RECIPES

The recipes in this chapter, both classic and new, are grouped according to type and shape of pasta. All express the genuine and direct approach to flavor that is characteristic of Italian cooking. You will find hot and cold dishes, soups, and even a dessert. Each recipe is presented with its ideal choice of pasta shape, with suggestions for suitable alternatives.

Each recipe serves 6 people if followed by a second course, or 4 people if served on its own

For a step-by-step guide to preparing vegetables, see pages 150–1

PASTA LUNGA

Long Pasta

SPAGHETTINI ALLE ERBE

Spaghettini with Garlic and Fresh Herbs

This is a good example of how bread crumbs are sometimes used with olive oil-based sauces to help the sauce cling to the pasta.

INGREDIENTS

For 1lb *spaghettini*

½ cup extra-virgin olive oil
1 tsp finely chopped garlic
2 Tbs finely chopped flat-leaf parsley
½ tsp finely chopped fresh rosemary
½ tsp finely chopped fresh thyme
salt and freshly ground black pepper
1 tsp shredded fresh basil
2 Tbs plain dried bread crumbs

PREPARATION

1 Bring 4 quarts of water to a boil in a large saucepan or pot, add 1 tablespoon of salt, and drop in the pasta all at once, stirring until the strands are submerged.
2 Put the olive oil and garlic in a large skillet over a medium-high heat and cook until the garlic begins to change color.
3 Stir in the parsley, rosemary, and thyme and season with salt and black pepper. After about 30 seconds, remove from the heat and set aside.
4 When the pasta is cooked *al dente*, drain it and add it to the sauce in the skillet, and return the skillet to a low heat.
5 Add the basil to the skillet and toss until the pasta is well coated with the sauce. Sprinkle the bread crumbs over the pasta, toss again, taste for salt and serve at once.

Also good with: *spaghetti*

SPAGHETTINI ALLA NURSINA

Spaghettini with Black Truffles

This dish is named after Norcia, a town in the heart of black-truffle country in central Italy. Although the white truffle from Alba is the aristocrat of truffles, the black truffle is certainly not to be scoffed at. I cannot think of a better way to eat spaghettini *than enveloped in the rich woodsy aroma and flavor of black truffles.*

INGREDIENTS

For 1lb *spaghettini*

½ cup extra-virgin olive oil
2 – 3 garlic cloves, lightly crushed and peeled but kept whole
2 anchovy fillets, finely chopped
4 – 5oz fresh **or**, if very good quality, preserved black truffles, finely grated
salt

PREPARATION

1 Bring 4 quarts of water to a boil in a large saucepan or pot, add 1 tablespoon of salt, and drop in the pasta all at once, stirring until the strands are submerged.
2 Put the olive oil and garlic in a large skillet over a medium-high heat and cook until the garlic has browned on all sides.
3 Remove and discard the garlic and turn the heat down to low. Allow the oil to cool slightly, then add the anchovies. Cook, stirring with a wooden spoon, until the anchovies have dissolved completely. Remove the skillet from the heat, stir in the truffles, and season very lightly with salt.
4 When the pasta is cooked *al dente*, drain it and toss thoroughly with the sauce. Taste for salt and serve at once.

Spaghettini ai Gamberi, Pomodoro e Capperi

Spaghettini with Shrimp, Tomatoes, and Capers

INGREDIENTS

For 1lb *spaghettini*

⅓ cup extra-virgin olive oil
1 cup yellow onion, thinly sliced lengthwise
1 lb fresh, ripe plum tomatoes, peeled, seeded
and cut into ½ in dice
½ tsp chopped fresh oregano **or** ¼ tsp dried
1½ Tbs capers
¾ lb fresh medium shrimp, peeled, deveined if
necessary, and cut into ½ in pieces
salt and freshly ground black pepper

PREPARATION

1 Put the olive oil and onion in a large skillet over a medium heat and cook until the onion has turned golden brown at the edges.
2 Raise the heat to medium-high and add the tomatoes. Cook rapidly until most of the liquid has evaporated but the tomatoes have not broken down completely. You may need to raise the heat even more but be careful not to burn them.
3 Meanwhile, bring 4 quarts of water to a boil in a large saucepan or pot, add 1 tablespoon of salt, and drop in the pasta all at once, stirring until the strands are submerged.
4 Add the oregano, capers and shrimp to the sauce in the skillet and season with salt and black pepper. Cook until the shrimp turn pink, about 2 minutes, then remove the skillet from the heat.
5 When the pasta is cooked *al dente*, drain it and toss it with the sauce. Serve at once.

Also good with: *spaghetti*

SPAGHETTINI ALLE OLIVE NERE

Spaghettini with Tomatoes and Black Olives

INGREDIENTS

For 1lb *spaghettini*

⅓ cup extra-virgin olive oil
2 tsps finely chopped garlic
2 Tbs finely chopped flat-leaf parsley
2 cups canned whole peeled tomatoes, with
their juice, coarsely chopped
salt and freshly ground black pepper
8 – 10 black olives, pitted and julienned

PREPARATION

1 Put the olive oil and garlic in a saucepan over a medium-high heat and cook until the garlic begins to change color.
2 Stir in the parsley then add the tomatoes. Season with salt and black pepper and cook until the tomatoes have reduced and separated from the oil. Remove from the heat and set aside.

You can prepare the sauce ahead of time up to this point and refrigerate or even freeze it.

3 Bring 4 quarts of water to a boil in a large saucepan or pot, add 1 tablespoon of salt, and drop in the pasta all at once, stirring until the strands are submerged.
4 Return the pan with the sauce to a low heat and mix in the olives.
5 When the pasta is cooked *al dente*, drain it and toss it with the sauce. Taste for salt and pepper and serve at once.

Also good with: *spaghetti*

SPAGHETTI AI GAMBERI E PEPERONI ARROSTO

Spaghetti with Shrimp and Roasted Bell Peppers

INGREDIENTS

For 1lb *spaghetti*

2 red bell peppers
3 Tbs extra-virgin olive oil
½ tsp finely chopped garlic
½ lb medium shrimp, peeled, deveined if
necessary, and cut into ½in pieces
salt and freshly ground black pepper
¾ cup heavy cream
1 Tb finely chopped flat-leaf parsley

PREPARATION

1 Roast the red bell peppers under the broiler or over an open flame until the skin is charred on all sides. Place them in a bowl and cover the bowl tightly with plastic wrap. After about 20 minutes take the peppers out, cut them in half, remove the core and scrape away the blistered skin and the seeds. Cut the flesh into ¾in squares.
2 Bring 4 quarts of water to a boil in a large saucepan or pot, add 1 tablespoon of salt and drop in the pasta all at once, stirring until the strands are submerged.
3 Put the olive oil and garlic in a large skillet over a medium-high heat and cook until the garlic begins to change color. Add the shrimp, season with salt and black pepper and sauté, stirring frequently, until the shrimp have turned pink: 1 – 2 minutes.
4 Stir in the roasted peppers and add the cream and the parsley. Cook until the cream has reduced by at least half, then remove the skillet from the heat and set aside.
5 When the pasta is cooked *al dente*, return the skillet with the sauce to a low heat, drain the pasta, and add it to the skillet. Toss the pasta over the heat until it is well coated. Serve at once.

Also good with: *fusilli lunghi, fettuccine*

SPAGHETTINI AI GAMBERI E FINOCCHIO

Spaghettini with Shrimp and Fresh Fennel

INGREDIENTS

For 1lb *spaghettini*

⅓ cup extra-virgin olive oil
2 tsps finely chopped garlic
3 cups fresh fennel, tops removed, bulbs sliced
very thinly lengthwise
1lb fresh ripe plum tomatoes, peeled, seeded
and cut into ½in dice
1 tsp chopped fresh marjoram **or** ½ tsp dried
¾ lb medium shrimp, peeled, deveined if necessary,
and cut into ½in pieces
salt and freshly ground black pepper

PREPARATION

1 Put the olive oil and garlic in a large skillet over a medium-high heat and cook until the garlic begins to change color. Stir in the fennel, coating it well with the oil, and add about ¼ cup of water. Turn the heat down to medium-low, cover the skillet and cook until the fennel is very tender: about 15 – 25 minutes.
2 Pour 4 quarts of water into a large saucepan or pot and place over a high heat.
3 Uncover the skillet with the fennel, raise the heat to medium-high, and cook until any water in the pan has evaporated. Stir in the tomatoes and cook briefly until their liquid has evaporated.
4 When the water for the pasta is boiling, add 1 tablespoon of salt and drop in the pasta all at once, stirring until the strands are submerged.
5 Add the marjoram and the shrimp to the sauce, season with salt and black pepper, and cook until the shrimp have turned pink: about 2 minutes. Remove the skillet from the heat and set aside.
6 When the pasta is cooked *al dente*, drain it and toss it with the sauce. Taste for salt and pepper and serve at once.

Also good with: *spaghetti, fusilli lunghi*

SPAGHETTI AL SUGO DI CIPOLLE VARIE

Spaghetti with Leeks, Shallots, and Red Onions

INGREDIENTS

For 1lb *spaghetti*

½ cup extra-virgin olive oil
4 Tbs thinly sliced shallots
2 cups red onions, thinly sliced
¾ lb leeks, green tops removed, cut into
thin strips 2in long
salt and freshly ground black pepper
¼ cup dry white wine
2 Tbs finely chopped flat-leaf parsley
⅓ cup freshly grated parmigiano-reggiano cheese

PREPARATION

1 Put the olive oil and shallots in a large skillet over a medium heat and cook until the shallots are lightly colored.
2 Stir in the onions and leeks, season generously with salt and black pepper, add ¼ cup water, turn the heat down to medium-low and cover the skillet. Cook until the onions and leeks have softened and become very tender: about 20 – 30 minutes.
3 Pour 4 quarts of water into a large saucepan or pot and place over a high heat.
4 Uncover the skillet with the sauce and raise the heat to medium-high. Cook, stirring occasionally, until any liquid in the pan has evaporated and the onions and leeks start to turn a rich golden color.
5 When the water for the pasta is boiling, add 1 tablespoon of salt, and drop in the pasta all at once, stirring until the strands are submerged.
6 Add the wine and parsley to the sauce and cook until the wine has evaporated almost completely. Remove the skillet from the heat and set aside.
7 When the pasta is cooked *al dente*, drain it and toss it with the sauce, adding the grated cheese. Taste for salt and pepper and serve at once.

Also good with: *spaghettini, tonnarelli, fusilli lunghi*

FUSILLI LUNGHI ALLA RUSTICA

Long Fusilli with Bell Peppers and Olives

This zesty, flavorful sauce is a recipe of my mother's that I am very fond of and have made minor changes to.

INGREDIENTS

For 1lb *fusilli lunghi*

½ cup extra-virgin olive oil
3 cups yellow onion, thinly sliced
1 tsp finely chopped garlic
½ tsp red pepper flakes
2 Tbs finely chopped flat-leaf parsley
3oz pancetta, *cut into thin strips from a* ¼*in thick slice*
1 large yellow or red bell pepper **or** ½ of each, cored and seeded, peeled and cut into strips ½in wide
1lb fresh ripe plum tomatoes, peeled, seeded and cut into ½in dice
salt
½ cup green olives, pitted and julienned
2 Tbs capers
1 tsp coarsely chopped fresh oregano **or** ½ tsp dried
2 Tbs fresh basil leaves, torn by hand into small pieces
4 Tbs freshly grated parmigiano-reggiano *cheese*
2 Tbs freshly grated pecorino romano *cheese*

PREPARATION

1 Put the olive oil and onion in a large skillet over a medium-low heat and cook until the onion has softened and turned a rich golden color.
2 Raise the heat to medium-high and stir in the garlic, red pepper flakes and parsley. Sauté for about 30 seconds. Add the *pancetta* and cook until it is lightly browned but not crisp.
3 Pour 4 quarts of water into a large saucepan or pot and place over a high heat.
4 Add the strips of bell pepper to the skillet with the sauce and cook, stirring occasionally, until they are tender: about 5–6 minutes. Add the tomatoes and cook until they are no longer watery: about another 5–6 minutes.
5 Season with salt, stir in the olives, capers, oregano, and basil, and after about 30 seconds remove the skillet from the heat and set aside.
6 When the water for the pasta is boiling, add 1 tablespoon of salt and drop in the pasta all at once, stirring until the strands are submerged.
7 When the pasta is cooked *al dente*, drain it and toss it with the sauce, adding the grated cheeses. Taste for salt and serve at once.

Also good with: *fusilli corti, penne, elicoidali*

Red bell pepper

Yellow bell pepper

Pancetta

Flat-leaf parsley

Red pepper flakes

Garlic

Onion

Extra-virgin olive oil

Plum
tomatoes

Salt

Green
olives

Capers

Oregano

Basil

Parmigiano-
reggiano

Pecorino
romano

Fusilli
lunghi

**Fusilli lunghi
alla rustica**

SPAGHETTI AI FRUTTI DI MARE

Spaghetti with Seafood Sauce

With two long coastlines, Italy has a wealth of seafood pasta dishes. This is one of the more common ones, a shellfish lover's delight that is found along both coasts, the Adriatic and the Mediterranean.

INGREDIENTS

For 1lb *spaghetti*

¾ lb squid
12 live small clams
12 live mussels
¼ lb bay scallops
¼ lb medium shrimp
⅓ cup extra-virgin olive oil, plus a little extra to add to the sauce
1 tsp finely chopped garlic
1 Tb finely chopped flat-leaf parsley
⅓ cup dry white wine
2 cups canned whole peeled tomatoes, with their juice, coarsely chopped
salt
⅛ tsp red pepper flakes

PREPARATION

1 Prepare the squid as shown, then cut the tentacles in half and the bodies into rings.
2 Clean the clams and mussels: soak them in water for 5 minutes, rinse them, and scrub the shells. Discard any that are open. Remove the beards from the mussels. Peel and devein the shrimp and cut in half.
3 Put the olive oil and garlic in a large skillet over a medium-high heat and cook until the garlic begins to sizzle. Then stir in the parsley and the squid, and continue stirring for 1 – 2 minutes.
4 Pour in the white wine and continue cooking until it has reduced by half.
5 Add the tomatoes and bring to a boil, then reduce the heat to low, partially cover the skillet with the lid, and simmer until the squid is very tender: about 45 minutes. If the liquid evaporates before the squid is done, pour in a little water.
6 When the squid is tender, add some salt (do not add salt before this point or the squid will become tough) and set the skillet aside.
7 Bring 4 quarts of water to a boil in a large saucepan or pot, add 1 tablespoon of salt, and drop in the pasta all at once, stirring until the strands are submerged.

PREPARING SQUID

1 *Rinse the squid first. Then remove the inner sac by pulling the head and body apart. The inner sac comes away with the head.*

8 Return the sauce to the heat and put in the red pepper flakes. Add the clams and mussels, and when they begin to open (after about 2 minutes), add the scallops and the shrimp. Season with salt, pour in a little extra olive oil, and cook for 2 – 3 minutes more. Set aside.
9 When the pasta is cooked *al dente*, drain it and toss it thoroughly with the sauce in a serving bowl, leaving the clams and mussels in their shells. Taste for salt and serve at once.

Clams

Shrimp

Mussel

Scallop

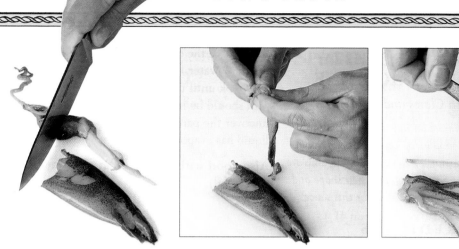

2 Detach the tentacles from the head and inner sac by cutting above the eyes. Keep the tentacles, which are edible, but discard the rest.

3 You need to remove the beak from the tentacles. Feel for the hard lump then gently work it out of the flesh by squeezing it.

4 Discard the transparent backbone then peel off the skin (this is easiest done under running water). Rinse again.

**Spaghetti ai
frutti di mare**

Spaghetti alle cozze
(page 81)

Bucatini alla sorrentina
(page 84)

Spaghetti al tonno fresco
(page 81)

SPAGHETTI ALLA CHECCA

Spaghetti with Fresh Tomatoes, Herbs, and Mozzarella

I discovered this refreshing summer dish at a restaurant called Cambusa in Positano, near Naples. It is another of those "uncooked" sauces where the ingredients are simply scalded with hot oil before being tossed with the pasta.

INGREDIENTS

For 1lb *spaghetti*

*2lbs fresh ripe plum tomatoes, peeled, seeded
and cut into ¼in dice
8oz whole-milk Italian mozzarella,
cut into ¼in dice
2 tsps chopped fresh basil
2 tsps chopped fresh oregano
2 tsps chopped fresh marjoram
1 tsp chopped fresh thyme
salt and freshly ground black pepper
½ cup extra-virgin olive oil*

PREPARATION

1 Bring 4 quarts of water to a boil in a large saucepan or pot, add 1 tablespoon of salt, and drop in the pasta all at once, stirring until the strands are submerged.
2 Meanwhile, put the tomatoes, *mozzarella* and all the herbs in a serving bowl large enough to accommodate the pasta later. Season with salt and black pepper and mix well.
3 Heat the olive oil until it is smoking hot and pour it over the mixture in the bowl.
4 When the pasta is cooked *molto al dente* (about 30 seconds away from being *al dente*), drain, and add it to the sauce in the bowl. Toss vigorously until the pasta is well coated. Cover the bowl with a plate and allow to stand for 2 minutes so the cheese melts before you serve it.

Also good with: *spaghettini*

Oregano

Basil

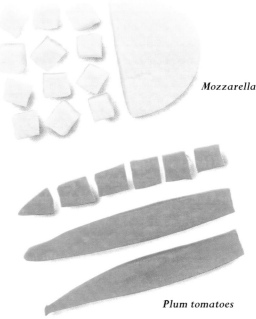

Mozzarella

Plum tomatoes

Marjoram

Thyme

Salt

Black
pepper

Extra-virgin
olive oil

Spaghetti

Spaghetti
alla checca

FUSILLI LUNGHI CON LA BELGA E PORRI

Long Fusilli with Belgian Endive, Leeks, and Roasted Bell Pepper

INGREDIENTS

For 1lb *fusilli lunghi*

1 red bell pepper
⅓ cup extra-virgin olive oil
1 tsp finely chopped garlic
3 medium-sized leeks, cut in half lengthwise
then across into pieces ¼in wide
1 cup Belgian endive, finely shredded lengthwise
salt and freshly ground black pepper

PREPARATION

1 Roast the red bell pepper under the broiler or over an open flame until the skin is charred on all sides. Place it in a bowl and cover the bowl tightly with plastic wrap. After about 20 minutes take the pepper out, cut it in half, remove the core and scrape away the blistered skin and the seeds. Cut into strips 1in long and ⅛in wide.
2 Put the olive oil and garlic in a large skillet over a medium-high heat. When the garlic begins to change color, add the leeks and Belgian endive. Season with salt and black pepper, and stir well to coat with the oil and garlic. Turn the heat down to medium-low, cover the skillet and cook, stirring occasionally, until the vegetables are very tender and almost creamy in texture: at least 20 minutes.
3 Meanwhile, bring 4 quarts of water to a boil in a large saucepan or pot, add 1 tablespoon of salt and drop in the pasta all at once, stirring until the strands are submerged.
4 Uncover the skillet, raise the heat to medium-high and add the strips of roasted pepper. Cook, stirring frequently, for 2–3 minutes then remove from the heat and set aside.
5 When the pasta is cooked *al dente*, drain it and toss it with the sauce. Taste for salt and pepper and serve at once.

Also good with: *spaghetti, gnocchi, conchiglie*

SPAGHETTI AL POMODORO

Spaghetti with Tomatoes, Carrots, and Celery

INGREDIENTS

For 1lb *spaghetti*

4 Tbs (½ stick) butter
¼ cup finely chopped yellow onion
¼ cup finely diced carrots
¼ cup finely diced celery
2 cups canned whole peeled tomatoes, with
their juice, coarsely chopped
salt
⅓ cup freshly grated parmigiano-reggiano cheese

PREPARATION

1 Melt the butter in a saucepan over a medium-low heat. Add the onion and cook until it has softened and turned a rich golden color. Add the carrots and celery and continue cooking until they are lightly colored.
2 Add the tomatoes, season with salt and cook until they have reduced and separated from the butter: about 20–30 minutes. Remove from the heat and set aside.

You can prepare the sauce ahead of time up to this point and refrigerate or even freeze it.

3 Bring 4 quarts of water to a boil, add 1 tablespoon of salt, and drop in the pasta all at once, stirring until the strands are submerged.
4 When the pasta is almost done, return the sauce to a medium heat. Once the pasta is cooked *al dente*, drain it and toss it with the sauce, adding the grated cheese. Taste for salt and serve at once.

Also good with: *penne, fusilli lunghi, fusilli corti, spaghettini*

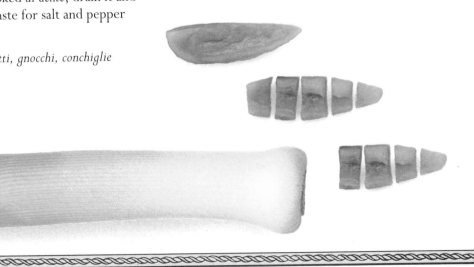

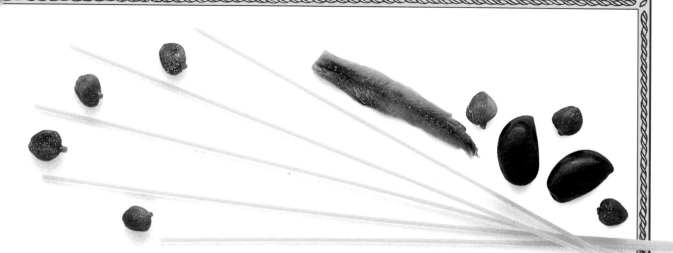

SPAGHETTI ALLA PUTTANESCA BIANCA

Spaghetti with Capers, Olives, and Anchovies

This is known as a "white" puttanesca *sauce because it is without tomatoes.*

INGREDIENTS

For 1lb *spaghetti*

½ cup extra-virgin olive oil
6 anchovy fillets, chopped
1 tsp finely chopped garlic
1 Tb finely chopped flat-leaf parsley
2 Tbs capers
8 – 10 black olives, pitted and julienned
salt
2 Tbs plain dried bread crumbs

PREPARATION

1 Bring 4 quarts of water to a boil in a large saucepan or pot, add 1 tablespoon of salt, and drop in the pasta all at once, stirring until the strands are submerged.
2 Put the olive oil and anchovies in a large skillet over a medium heat and cook, stirring with a wooden spoon, until the anchovies have dissolved.
3 Add the garlic and sauté until it just begins to change color.
4 Stir in the parsley, capers, and olives, season with a little salt and cook for 1–2 minutes. Remove from the heat and set aside.
5 When the pasta is cooked *al dente*, drain it and toss it with the sauce, adding the bread crumbs. Taste for salt and serve at once.

Also good with: *spaghettini*

SPAGHETTI AL COGNAC

Spaghetti with Fresh Tomatoes and Cognac

This dish was invented by Alfredo, the famous Roman chef who created Fettuccine all'Alfredo. *It is traditionally eaten in Rome at 4 a.m.*

INGREDIENTS

For 1lb *spaghetti*

⅓ cup extra-virgin olive oil
1 cup finely chopped yellow onion
2 Tbs cognac
1lb fresh ripe plum tomatoes, peeled, seeded and cut into ¼ in dice
salt and freshly ground black pepper

PREPARATION

1 Put the olive oil and onion in a large skillet over a medium heat and cook until the onion has softened and turned a rich golden color.
2 Turn the heat up to medium-high and pour in the cognac. Cook for about 30 seconds to allow the alcohol to evaporate, then add the tomatoes. Season with salt and black pepper and cook, stirring occasionally, until the tomatoes have reduced and separated from the oil: about 10–20 minutes. Remove from the heat and set aside.
3 Bring 4 quarts of water to a boil in a large saucepan or pot, add 1 tablespoon of salt, and drop in the pasta all at once, stirring until the strands are submerged.
4 When the pasta is cooked *al dente*, return the skillet with the sauce to a low heat, drain the pasta and add it to the skillet. Toss over the heat until the pasta is well coated. Serve at once, grinding some fresh black pepper over each serving.

Also good with: *spaghettini, penne*

FETTUCCE

Ribbons

TAGLIOLINI ALLA ROMAGNOLA

Tagliolini with Prosciutto

This is a classic example of how simple good Italian food can be. Handmade egg noodles, good quality prosciutto, parmigiano-reggiano, and butter are all you need to make this wonderful dish. The only possible improvement would be the addition of fresh early peas.

INGREDIENTS

For *tagliolini* made with 3 eggs (see page 36) or 1lb dried, store-bought egg *tagliolini*

1 cup fresh shelled peas (optional)
6 Tbs (¾ stick) butter
4oz prosciutto, *cut into thin strips from a ¼in thick slice*
½ cup freshly grated parmigiano-reggiano *cheese*

PREPARATION

1 If using peas, cook them in boiling salted water until tender. Drain and set aside.
2 Pour 4 quarts of water into a large saucepan or pot and place over a high heat.
3 Melt the butter in a large skillet over a medium-high heat. Add the *prosciutto* and sauté until it is lightly browned: 2–3 minutes. If using peas, add them now and sauté for 5 more minutes. Remove from the heat and set aside.
4 When the water for the pasta is boiling, and the sauce is off the heat, add 1 tablespoon of salt to the boiling water and drop in the pasta all at once, stirring well.
5 When the pasta is cooked *al dente*, drain it and toss it with the sauce, adding the grated cheese. Serve at once.

Also good with: *fettuccine, tagliatelle*

FETTUCCINE ALLE ERBE E PANNA ROSA

Fettuccine with Herbs, Fresh Tomatoes, and Cream

You need fresh herbs and the best-quality ripe plum tomatoes you can find for this recipe.

INGREDIENTS

For *fettuccine* made with 3 eggs (see page 36) or 1lb dried, store-bought egg *fettuccine*

4 Tbs (½ stick) butter
2 tsps finely chopped fresh basil
1 tsp finely chopped fresh rosemary
1 tsp finely chopped fresh sage
½ beef bouillon cube
2lbs fresh ripe plum tomatoes, peeled, seeded, and cut into ¼in dice
salt and freshly ground black pepper
½ cup heavy cream

PREPARATION

1 Pour 4 quarts of water into a large saucepan or pot and place over a high heat.
2 Melt the butter in a large skillet over a medium heat. Add all the herbs and the bouillon cube and stir with a wooden spoon, until the cube has dissolved completely: about 1 minute. Be careful not to let the butter burn.
3 Add the tomatoes, season with salt and black pepper and cook until they have reduced and separated from the butter: 5–10 minutes.
4 Raise the heat to medium-high and pour in the cream. Cook, stirring frequently, until it has reduced by about half, then remove the skillet from the heat and set aside.
5 When the water for the pasta is boiling, and the sauce is off the heat, add 1 tablespoon of salt to the boiling water and drop in the pasta all at once, stirring well.
6 When the pasta is cooked *al dente*, drain it and toss it with the sauce. Serve at once.

Also good with: *tagliatelle* (*spaghetti* is acceptable but only as a last resort)

FETTUCCINE ALLE ZUCCHINE E ZAFFERANO

Fettuccine with Zucchini and Saffron Cream

In this elegant sauce the cream takes on the flavor of the saffron and zucchini. It is perfectly suited to homemade egg pasta.

INGREDIENTS

For *fettuccine* made with 3 eggs (see page 36) or 1lb dried, store-bought egg *fettuccine*

4 Tbs (½ stick) butter
½ cup finely chopped yellow onion
1½ lbs zucchini, cut into sticks 1½ in long and ¼ in thick
salt and freshly ground black pepper
1 cup heavy cream
¼ tsp finely chopped saffron strands
⅓ cup freshly grated parmigiano-reggiano *cheese*

PREPARATION

1 Pour 4 quarts of water into a large saucepan or pot and place over a high heat.
2 Melt the butter in a large skillet over a medium heat. Add the onion and cook until it has has softened and turned a rich golden color.
3 Raise the heat to medium-high and add the zucchini. Cook until they are tender and lightly browned. Season with salt and black pepper.
4 Pour in the cream and add the saffron. Cook, stirring frequently, until the cream has reduced by half. Remove from the heat.
5 When the water for the pasta is boiling, and the sauce is off the heat, add 1 tablespoon of salt to the boiling water and drop in the pasta all at once, stirring well.
6 When the pasta is cooked *al dente*, drain it and toss it with the sauce, adding the grated cheese. Serve at once.

Also good with: *tagliatelle*

FETTUCCINE AL TONNO E PANNA ALLO ZAFFERANO

Fettuccine with Fresh Tuna and Saffron Cream

Fresh tuna dries out very quickly if overcooked. Sear it briefly before adding the cream to keep it moist.

INGREDIENTS

For *fettuccine* made with 3 eggs (see page 36) or 1lb dried, store-bought egg *fettuccine*

2 Tbs butter
½ tsp finely chopped garlic
½ lb fresh tuna, cut into ½ in chunks
salt and freshly ground black pepper
1 cup heavy cream
¼ tsp finely chopped saffron strands
1 Tb finely chopped flat-leaf parsley

PREPARATION

1 Pour 4 quarts of water into a large saucepan or pot and place over a high heat.
2 Melt the butter in a large skillet over a medium-high heat. Add the garlic and cook until it begins to sizzle.
3 Stir in the tuna and cook until it loses its raw color: about 2 minutes. Season with salt and black pepper.
4 Pour in the cream and add the saffron. Cook, stirring frequently, until the cream has reduced by half, stir in the parsley, and remove the skillet from the heat.
5 When the water for the pasta is boiling, and the sauce is off the heat, add 1 tablespoon of salt to the boiling water and drop in the pasta all at once, stirring well.
6 When the pasta is cooked *al dente*, return the sauce to a low heat, drain the pasta and toss it with the sauce. Serve at once.

Also good with: *tagliatelle*

FETTUCCINE ALLE VERDURE

Fettuccine with Vegetables and Roasted Red Pepper Sauce

This is a great dish for health-conscious vegetarians. Instead of cream I use a purée of roasted red peppers to bind the ingredients together.

INGREDIENTS

For *fettuccine* made with 3 eggs (see page 36) or 1lb dried, store-bought egg *fettuccine*

2 red bell peppers
2 Tbs butter, softened to room temperature
salt and freshly ground black pepper
¼ cup extra-virgin olive oil
1 tsp finely chopped garlic
2 cups eggplant, peeled and cut into ½ in dice
2 cups zucchini, cut into ½ in dice
1 yellow bell pepper, cored and seeded, peeled, and cut into ½ in squares
¼ cup freshly grated parmigiano-reggiano cheese

PREPARATION

1 Roast the red bell peppers under the broiler or over an open flame until the skin is charred on all sides. Place them in a bowl and cover the bowl tightly with plastic wrap. After about 20 minutes take the peppers out, cut them in half, remove the core and scrape away the blistered skin and the seeds. Place the peppers in a food processor with the butter, season with salt and black pepper, and grind until creamy. Remove and set aside.
2 Pour 4 quarts of water into a large saucepan or pot and place over a high heat.
3 Put the olive oil and the garlic in a large skillet over a medium heat and cook until the garlic begins to sizzle.
4 Add the eggplant, zucchini, and yellow bell pepper and stir until well coated (do not worry if the eggplant soaks up all the oil, it will release it once it is cooked). Cover the skillet and cook until the vegetables are tender: 10–15 minutes.
5 Stir the red pepper sauce into the vegetables. Remove from the heat and set aside.
6 When the water for the pasta is boiling, and the sauce is off the heat, add 1 tablespoon of salt to the boiling water and drop in the pasta all at once, stirring well.
7 When the pasta is cooked *al dente*, drain it and toss it with the sauce, adding the grated cheese. Serve at once.

Also good with: *tagliatelle*

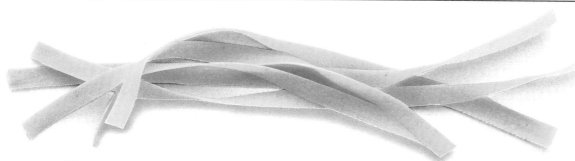

FETTUCCINE COI FICHI SECCHI

Fettuccine with Dried Figs

This is definitely a recipe for the adventurous. I would not recommend serving it as a main meal, but rather as a starter, before roast duck for example. In Rome a small dish of spaghetti with oil and garlic is sometimes served at the end of the meal — fettuccine with figs would also make the perfect ending, served to 6–8 people.

INGREDIENTS

**For *fettuccine* made with 3 eggs (see page 36)
or 1lb dried, store-bought egg *fettuccine***

*6oz dried figs
4 Tbs (½ stick) butter
1 Tb grappa or brandy
1 cup heavy cream
salt and freshly ground black pepper
⅓ cup freshly grated parmigiano-reggiano cheese*

PREPARATION

1 Place the figs in a bowl, cover with lukewarm water and soak for at least 30 minutes. Drain, reserving the soaking water, and cut the figs into pieces of about ⅛–¼ in.
2 Pour 4 quarts of water into a large saucepan or pot and place over a high heat.
3 Melt the butter in a skillet over a medium-high heat. Add the figs and cook for 1–2 minutes.
4 Pour in the *grappa* or brandy and let the alcohol bubble away (this will take about 1 minute). Add about ¼ cup of the soaking water from the figs and cook until it has evaporated.
5 Add the cream, season generously with salt and black pepper, and cook, stirring frequently, until the cream has reduced by half. Remove from the heat and set aside.
6 When the water for the pasta is boiling, and the sauce is off the heat, add 1 tablespoon of salt to the boiling water and drop in the pasta all at once, stirring well.
7 When the pasta is cooked *al dente*, drain it and toss it with the sauce, adding the grated cheese. Serve at once.

FETTUCCINE AL GORGONZOLA

Fettuccine with Gorgonzola Cheese

This is the classic gorgonzola sauce found in northern Italy. The gorgonzola required is dolce, the creamy, almost runny kind as opposed to the drier, sharper one. For an interesting variation, try tossing in a couple of tablespoons of toasted pine nuts at the end.

INGREDIENTS

**For *fettuccine* made with 3 eggs (see page 36)
or 1lb dried, store-bought egg *fettuccine***

*4oz Italian gorgonzola dolce
(see introductory note above)
½ cup whole milk
2 Tbs butter
salt
⅓ cup heavy cream
⅓ cup freshly grated parmigiano-reggiano cheese*

PREPARATION

1 Pour 4 quarts of water into a large saucepan or pot and place over a high heat.
2 Put the *gorgonzola*, milk, butter, and a pinch of salt in a large skillet over a low heat. Cook, breaking up the cheese with a wooden spoon until it has melted completely and formed a thick creamy sauce.
3 Pour in the cream and raise the heat to medium-high. Cook, stirring frequently, until the cream has reduced to two-thirds of its original volume (this will take 3–5 minutes). Remove the skillet from the heat and set aside.
4 When the water for the pasta is boiling, and the sauce is off the heat, add 1 tablespoon of salt to the boiling water and drop in the pasta all at once, stirring well.
5 When the pasta is cooked *al dente*, drain and transfer to the skillet with the sauce. Turn the heat on low and toss the pasta over the heat with the sauce and the grated cheese for about 30 seconds. Serve at once.

Also good with: *spaghettini, spaghetti, garganelli, penne*

FETTUCCINE ALL'ARANCIO

Fettuccine with Orange and Mint

The idea for this came from Lori Vorst, a very good cook I've worked with. It is unusual but simple and refreshing.

INGREDIENTS

For *fettuccine* made with 3 eggs (see page 36)
or* 1lb dried, store-bought egg *fettuccine

6 Tbs (¾ stick) butter
2 tsps finely chopped orange zest
1 tsp finely shredded fresh mint
salt and freshly ground black pepper
½ cup freshly squeezed orange juice
½ cup freshly grated parmigiano-reggiano cheese

PREPARATION

1 Pour 4 quarts of water into a large saucepan or pot and place over a high heat.
2 Melt the butter in a large skillet over a medium-high heat. Stir in the orange zest and mint and season with salt and black pepper.
3 Pour in the orange juice and cook until it has reduced to about two-thirds of its volume and has thickened slightly. Remove the skillet from the heat.
4 When the water for the pasta is boiling, and the sauce is off the heat, add 1 tablespoon of salt to the boiling water and drop in the pasta all at once, stirring well.
5 When the pasta is cooked *al dente*, drain it and toss it with the sauce, adding the grated cheese. Serve at once.

FETTUCCINE AL TARTUFO BIANCO

Fettuccine with White Truffles

If I were condemned to death and had to choose a last meal before my execution, it would be this dish, made with hand-rolled fettuccine and generous shavings of Italian white truffles.

INGREDIENTS

For *fettuccine* made with 3 eggs (see page 36),
preferably hand-rolled

6 Tbs (¾ stick) butter, cut into cubes
¼ cup freshly grated parmigiano-reggiano cheese
2oz, at least, of fresh white truffles

PREPARATION

1 Bring 4 quarts of water to a boil in a large saucepan or pot, add 1½ tablespoons of salt, and drop in the pasta all at once, stirring well.
2 When the pasta is cooked *al dente*, drain it and place it in a heated serving platter with the butter and the freshly grated cheese. Toss well and serve at once, shaving the truffles as thinly as possible over each plate using a peeler or, if you have one, a truffle shaver.

Also good with: *tagliatelle*

Fettuccine all'arancio

Fettuccine al Prosciutto e Asparagi

Fettuccine with Prosciutto, Asparagus, and Cream

INGREDIENTS

For *fettuccine* made with 3 eggs (see page 36) *or* 1lb dried, store-bought egg *fettuccine*

½ lb asparagus
salt
3 Tbs butter
½ cup finely chopped yellow onion
4oz prosciutto, *cut into thin strips from an ⅛in thick slice*
1 cup heavy cream
½ cup freshly grated parmigiano-reggiano *cheese*

PREPARATION

1 Trim and peel the lower green portions of the asparagus. Cook whole in salted boiling water in a skillet until tender.

2 Reserve ½ cup of the water. Cut the asparagus, when cool enough to handle, into ¾in lengths.

3 Pour 4 quarts of water into a large saucepan or pot and place over a high heat.

4 Melt the butter in a skillet over a medium heat. Add the onion and cook until it softens and turns a rich golden color. Stir in the *prosciutto* and sauté until it has lost its raw color.

5 Add the asparagus, raise the heat to medium-high and cook until it is lightly colored. Pour the reserved water in and cook until it has evaporated.

6 Stir in the cream and cook, stirring frequently, until it has reduced by half. Remove the skillet from the heat and set aside.

7 When the water for the pasta is boiling, and the sauce is off the heat, add 1 tablespoon of salt to the boiling water and drop in the pasta all at once, stirring well.

8 When the pasta is cooked *al dente*, drain it and toss it with the sauce, adding the grated cheese. Serve at once.

Also good with: *penne, fusilli corti, garganelli*

FETTUCCINE AL LIMONE

Fettuccine with Lemon

This is a dish you have to taste to believe. When my mother wrote this recipe for her third book, she could not have dreamt how many people would become fans of it. This recipe is like the original, with minor adjustments.

INGREDIENTS

For *fettuccine* made with 3 eggs (see page 36) or 1lb dried, store-bought egg *fettuccine*

3 Tbs butter
2 Tbs freshly squeezed lemon juice
1 tsp finely chopped lemon zest
1 cup heavy cream
salt and freshly ground black pepper
½ cup freshly grated parmigiano-reggiano *cheese*

PREPARATION

1 Pour 4 quarts of water into a large saucepan or pot and place over a high heat.
2 Put the butter, lemon juice, and zest in a large skillet over a medium-high heat. Once the butter has melted, let the lemon and butter bubble for about 30 seconds.
3 Pour in the cream. Season with salt and black pepper and cook, stirring frequently, until the cream has reduced by half. Remove the skillet from the heat and set aside.
4 When the water for the pasta is boiling, and the sauce is off the heat, add 1 tablespoon of salt to the boiling water and drop in the pasta all at once, stirring well.
5 When the pasta is cooked *al dente*, drain it and transfer it to the skillet with the sauce. Turn the heat on to medium and toss the pasta over the heat with the sauce and the grated cheese for about 15 seconds. Serve at once.

TRENETTE AL PESTO DI NOCI

Trenette with Walnut Pesto

Walnut pesto, like basil pesto, is a speciality of Liguria on the Italian Riviera. It is good with fettuccine (known as trenette *in Liguria) and is also traditionally served with* pansoti, *a triangular pasta parcel filled with five different local wild greens.*

INGREDIENTS

For *trenette* (*fettuccine*) made with 3 eggs (see page 36) or 1lb dried, store-bought egg *fettuccine*

½ lb shelled walnuts
1 tsp finely chopped garlic
2 Tbs extra-virgin olive oil
¼ cup whole-milk ricotta
salt
¼ cup heavy cream
¼ cup freshly grated parmigiano-reggiano *cheese*

PREPARATION

1 Pour 4 quarts of water into a large saucepan or pot and place over a high heat.
2 Put the walnuts and garlic in a food processor or blender and chop as finely as possible. Pour in the olive oil and process until well mixed. Add the *ricotta*, season with salt, and process again.
3 Transfer the mixture to a serving bowl and add the cream, mixing well with a wooden spoon.
4 When the water for the pasta is boiling, add 1 tablespoon of salt and drop in the pasta all at once, stirring well.
5 When the pasta is cooked *al dente*, put 4 tablespoons of the boiling water in the serving bowl with the walnut sauce, then drain the pasta. Toss the pasta in the serving bowl with the sauce, adding the grated cheese. Serve at once.

Also good with: *pansoti* (see introductory note above), *spaghetti*

I PIZZOCCHERI DELLA VALTELLINA

*Buckwheat Noodles with Fontina and
Swiss Chard*

*Pizzoccheri are buckwheat noodles, a speciality of the
Valtellina region in northern Italy. You can find them
sold dried in specialty food stores.*

INGREDIENTS

4 Tbs (½ stick) butter
4 whole garlic cloves, lightly crushed and peeled
3 – 4 fresh sage leaves
salt
1lb pizzoccheri
*½ lb new potatoes, peeled and cut
into slices ¼ in thick*
*1 cup Swiss chard stalks cut into sticks 1 in long
and ½ in wide* **and** *1 cup Swiss chard leaves
torn into small pieces*
4oz Italian fontina *cheese, cut into thin slivers*
½ cup freshly grated parmigiano-reggiano *cheese*

PREPARATION

1 Preheat the oven to 400°F.
2 Melt the butter in a small saucepan over a
medium-high heat. Add the garlic and the sage and
cook until the garlic has lightly browned on all
sides. Remove the pan from the heat and set aside.
3 Bring 4 quarts of water to a boil in a large
saucepan or pot. Put in 1 tablespoon of salt, the
pasta and the potatoes and cook for 8 minutes,
adding, after 5 minutes, the Swiss chard stalks.
4 Drop in the Swiss chard leaves and, when the
water returns to a boil, cook for about 1 minute.
By this time the pasta should be *al dente*.
5 Drain the pasta and vegetables and transfer
them to a mixing bowl. Pour the butter through a
strainer over them and add three-quarters of the
fontina and half the grated cheese. Toss well and
transfer to a buttered baking dish. Sprinkle the
remaining cheeses on top.
6 Bake on the upper rack of the oven for about
5 minutes. Remove the baking dish and allow the
pasta to rest for 2 – 3 minutes before serving.

TAGLIATELLE COI GAMBERI E ASPARAGI

Tagliatelle with Shrimp and Asparagus

INGREDIENTS

For *tagliatelle* **made with 3 eggs (see page 36)**
or 1lb dried, store-bought egg *tagliatelle*

¾ lb asparagus
¼ cup extra-virgin olive oil
1 Tb finely chopped garlic
¾ lb medium shrimp, peeled, deveined if necessary,
and cut into ½ in pieces
salt and freshly ground black pepper
2 Tbs butter, at room temperature

PREPARATION

1 Trim and peel the lower green portions of the asparagus. Cook whole in salted boiling water in a skillet until tender. Reserve the cooking water, and when the asparagus are cool enough to handle, cut them into 1in lengths.
2 Pour 4 quarts of water into a large saucepan or pot and place over a high heat.
3 Put the olive oil and garlic in a large skillet over a medium-high heat and cook until the garlic begins to sizzle.
4 Add the asparagus and cook, stirring frequently, for 2–3 minutes, or less if the garlic starts to brown. Pour in ½ cup of the asparagus water and cook until it has reduced by half.
5 Stir in the shrimp, season generously with black pepper and cook until they have all turned pink. The sauce should be slightly runny: if necessary add a little more asparagus water. Taste for salt and remove from the heat.
6 When the water for the pasta is boiling, add 1 tablespoon of salt and drop in the pasta all at once, stirring well.
7 When the pasta is cooked *al dente*, drain it and toss it thoroughly with the sauce and the butter. Serve at once.

TAGLIATELLE COI CECI

Tagliatelle with Chickpeas and Tomatoes

INGREDIENTS

For *tagliatelle* **made with 3 eggs (see page 36)**
or 1lb dried, store-bought egg *tagliatelle*

⅓ cup extra-virgin olive oil
½ cup finely chopped yellow onion
1 tsp finely chopped garlic
1 cup canned whole peeled tomatoes, with
their juice, coarsely chopped
1 tsp fresh rosemary *or* ½ tsp dried, finely chopped
salt and freshly ground black pepper
1½ cups drained canned chickpeas
¼ cup freshly grated parmigiano-reggiano *cheese*

PREPARATION

1 Put the olive oil and onion in a large skillet over a medium heat and cook until the onion softens and turns a rich golden color.
2 Add the garlic and continue cooking until it begins to change color.
3 Add the tomatoes and rosemary, season with salt and black pepper, and cook until the tomatoes have reduced and separated from the oil: about 10–20 minutes.
4 Pour 4 quarts of water into a large saucepan or pot and place over a high heat.
5 Add the chickpeas to the sauce in the skillet and cook for another 5 minutes. Using a slotted spoon, take out about half of the chickpeas. Purée them through a food mill or mash them with a fork and return them to the skillet. Cook for another minute, stirring, then remove the skillet from the heat and set aside.
6 When the water for the pasta is boiling, add 1 tablespoon of salt and drop in the pasta all at once, stirring well.
7 When the pasta is cooked *al dente*, drain it and toss it with the sauce, adding the grated cheese. Serve at once.

Also good with: *tonnarelli*

PAGLIA E FIENO COI PISELLI

*Yellow and Green Fettuccine with Peas,
Prosciutto, and Cream*

*The yellow and green noodles for this dish are
called* paglia e fieno, *which means "straw and hay."
In this version peas and* prosciutto *provide
a contrast of sweet and savory flavors.*

INGREDIENTS

**For *paglia e fieno* made with 3 eggs (see page 36)
or 1lb dried, store-bought egg *paglia e fieno***

¾ lb fresh shelled peas **or** *a 10oz package
of frozen tiny peas, thawed*
4 Tbs (½ stick) butter
¼ cup finely chopped yellow onion
4oz prosciutto, *cut into thin strips
from a ¼ in thick slice*
salt and freshly ground black pepper
1 cup heavy cream
½ cup freshly grated parmigiano-reggiano *cheese*

PREPARATION

1 If using fresh peas, cook them in boiling
salted water until tender. Drain and set aside.
2 Pour 4 quarts of water into a large saucepan or
pot and place over a high heat.
3 Melt the butter in a large skillet over a medium-
low heat. Add the onion and cook until it has
softened and turned a rich golden color. Add the
prosciutto and continue cooking, stirring, until it
has lost its raw color: 1 – 2 minutes.
4 Raise the heat to medium-high and add the
cooked fresh peas or the thawed frozen ones.
Season lightly with salt and black pepper
(remembering that the *prosciutto* is already salty)
and cook, stirring occasionally, for 2 – 3 minutes.
5 Pour in the cream and cook, stirring
frequently, until it has reduced by half. Remove
the skillet from the heat and set aside.
6 When the water for the pasta is boiling, and
the sauce is off the heat, add 1 tablespoon of salt
to the boiling water and drop in the pasta all at
once, stirring well.
7 When the pasta is cooked *al dente*, drain it and
toss it with the sauce, adding the grated cheese.
Taste for salt and serve at once.

PAGLIA E FIENO AI FUNGHI

*Yellow and Green Fettuccine with Mushrooms,
Ham, and Cream*

*Paglia e fieno is sometimes served with mushrooms
instead of peas. Ham is used here because
its milder flavor is better suited to mushrooms
than prosciutto is.*

INGREDIENTS

**For *paglia e fieno* made with 3 eggs (see page 36)
or 1lb dried, store-bought egg *paglia e fieno***

4 Tbs (½ stick) butter
¼ cup finely chopped yellow onion
*4oz boiled ham, cut into thin strips
from a ¼ in thick slice*
*¾ lb fresh white mushrooms, cleaned and
cut into ½ in dice*
salt and freshly ground black pepper
1 cup heavy cream
½ cup freshly grated parmigiano-reggiano *cheese*

PREPARATION

1 Pour 4 quarts of water into a large saucepan or
pot and place over a high heat.
2 Melt the butter in a large skillet over a
medium-low heat. Add the onion and cook until
it has softened and turned a rich golden color.
Add the ham and continue cooking, stirring,
until it is lightly colored: 1 – 2 minutes.
3 Raise the heat to medium-high and add the
mushrooms. Season lightly with salt and black
pepper (remembering that the ham is already
salty) and cook, stirring occasionally, until all the
water the mushrooms give off has evaporated.
Continue cooking for 4 – 5 minutes longer.
4 Pour in the cream and cook, stirring
frequently, until it has reduced by half. Remove
the skillet from the heat and set aside.
5 When the water for the pasta is boiling, and
the sauce is off the heat, add 1 tablespoon of salt
to the boiling water and drop in the pasta all at
once, stirring well.
6 When the pasta is cooked *al dente*, drain it
it and toss it with the sauce in the skillet,
adding the grated cheese. Taste for salt and
serve at once.

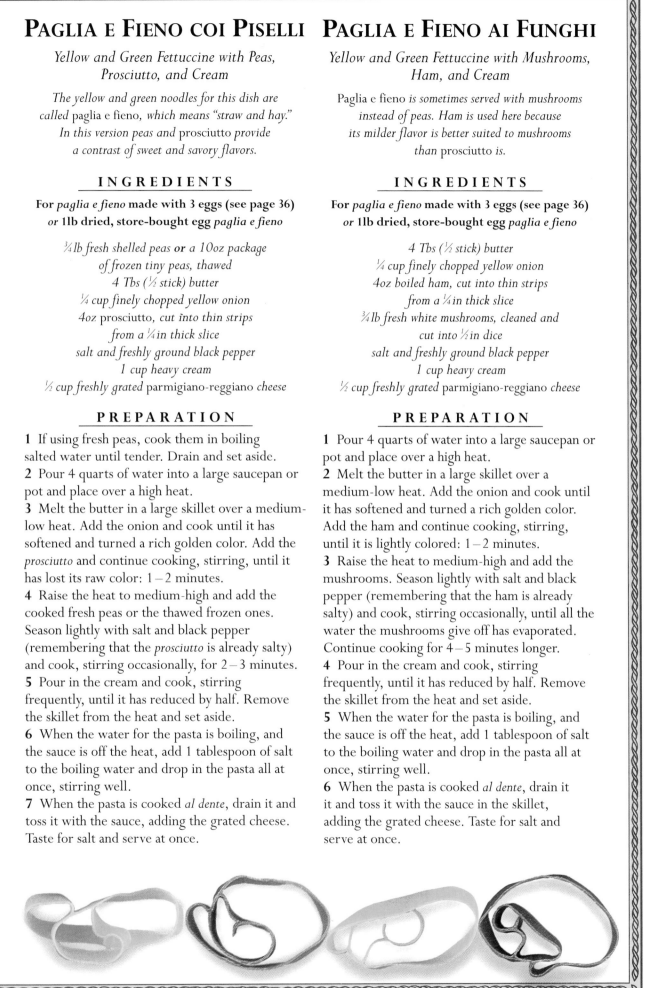

Pappardelle al coniglio
(page 103)

Tonnarelli al
radicchio e belga
(page 103)

Paglia e fieno coi
piselli (page 99)

PAPPARDELLE AL SUGO DI PICCIONE

Pappardelle with Squab

It was always a special treat when my mother made pan-roasted squab (young pigeon) for the family. I've adapted her recipe into a sauce for pasta.

INGREDIENTS

For *pappardelle* made with 3 eggs (see page 36) *or* 1lb dried, store-bought egg *pappardelle*

2 squab, about 1lb each
2 thin slices of pancetta
12 fresh sage leaves, 8 finely chopped and 4 whole
3 Tbs butter
2 Tbs vegetable oil
salt and freshly ground black pepper
½ cup dry white wine
⅓ cup freshly grated parmigiano-reggiano *cheese*

PREPARATION

1 Remove the organs from the birds' cavities and save the livers. Wash the squab under cold running water and pat them dry. Put a slice of *pancetta*, the liver and 2 whole sage leaves inside each bird.
2 Put a tablespoon of the butter and all the vegetable oil in a large, deep skillet over a medium-high heat. Allow the butter to foam and, when it begins to subside, put in the squab and the chopped sage. Brown the birds on all sides.
3 Season with salt and black pepper, then pour in the white wine and let it bubble for about 30 seconds. Turn the heat down to medium-low and cover the skillet. Cook, turning the squab every 15 minutes, until very tender: about 1 hour.
4 Remove the birds from the skillet and allow them to cool. Remove all the meat from the bones and cut it into pieces no larger than ¾in. Finely chop the livers and the *pancetta*.
5 Skim any excess fat from the juices in the skillet and return the meat, livers and *pancetta* to it. Cook over a medium-high heat until the sauce has reduced and is no longer watery. Remove the skillet from the heat and set aside.

You can prepare the sauce ahead of time up to this point and refrigerate it.

6 Bring 4 quarts of water to a boil in a large saucepan or pot, add 1 tablespoon of salt and drop in the pasta all at once, stirring well.
7 When the pasta is cooked *al dente*, drain it and toss it with the sauce, the remaining 2 tablespoons of butter, and the grated cheese. Serve at once.

PAPPARDELLE COI FEGATINI DI POLLO

Pappardelle with Chicken Livers

This is a classic Tuscan dish. My favorite recipe for it is my mother's, to which I have made very minor changes.

INGREDIENTS

For *pappardelle* made with 3 eggs (see page 36) *or* 1lb dried, store-bought egg *pappardelle*

2 Tbs extra-virgin olive oil
2 Tbs butter
2 Tbs finely chopped shallots
½ tsp finely chopped garlic
2oz pancetta, *finely diced*
1 tsp chopped fresh sage or ½ tsp dried
¼ lb ground beef
½ lb chicken livers, trimmed of any fat and cut into approximately ½in pieces
salt and freshly ground black pepper
2 tsps tomato paste
¼ cup dry white vermouth
⅓ cup freshly grated parmigiano-reggiano *cheese*

PREPARATION

1 Put the olive oil, butter, and shallots in a saucepan over a medium heat and sauté until the shallots begin to color.
2 Stir in the garlic and, after about 30 seconds, the *pancetta* and sage. Cook until the *pancetta* begins to brown lightly.
3 Add the ground beef and cook, breaking it up with a wooden spoon, until it loses its raw color.
4 Add the chicken livers, season with salt and black pepper and cook for a few more minutes until they have lost their raw color.
5 Pour 4 quarts of water into a large saucepan or pot and place over a high heat.
6 Dissolve the tomato paste in the vermouth. Raise the heat to medium-high under the sauce, pour in the vermouth and cook, stirring frequently, until most of the liquid has evaporated: 5–10 minutes. Remove the pan from the heat.
7 When the water for the pasta is boiling, and the sauce is off the heat, add 1 tablespoon of salt to the boiling water and drop in the pasta all at once, stirring well.
8 When the pasta is cooked *al dente*, drain it and toss it with the sauce, adding the grated cheese. Serve at once.

Also good with: *tagliatelle*

PAPPARDELLE AL CONIGLIO

Pappardelle with Rabbit

Pappardelle *with hare sauce is a classic Tuscan dish. Since it can be difficult to find wild hare, I've adapted the recipe for rabbit, a milder meat.*

INGREDIENTS

For *pappardelle* made with 3 eggs (see page 36) *or* 1lb dried, store-bought egg *pappardelle*

3 Tbs extra-virgin olive oil
3 Tbs butter
¼ cup finely chopped yellow onion
¼ cup finely diced carrot
¼ cup finely diced celery
¾ lb boneless rabbit meat, cut into
cubes no larger than ½ in
1 tsp finely chopped fresh rosemary **or** ½ tsp dried
2 Tbs juniper berries
1 cup dry red wine
1½ cups canned whole peeled tomatoes, with
their juice, coarsely chopped
salt and freshly ground black pepper
½ cup freshly grated parmigiano-reggiano *cheese*

PREPARATION

1 Put the olive oil, a third of the butter, and all the onion in a heavy-bottomed, deep saucepan over a medium heat and sauté until the onion has turned a light golden color.
2 Add the carrot and celery and cook until they begin to change color: 5–10 minutes.
3 Stir in the rabbit, rosemary, and juniper berries and cook until the meat has browned lightly.
4 Turn the heat up to medium-high and pour in the red wine. After about 2 minutes, when the alcohol from the wine has bubbled away, add the tomatoes and season with salt and black pepper.
5 When the tomatoes begin to bubble, reduce the heat to low and cook until the rabbit is very tender: at least 1 hour. If all the liquid evaporates before the rabbit is fully tender, add a little water. When done, remove the pan from the heat.

You can prepare the sauce ahead of time up to this point and refrigerate it.

6 Bring 4 quarts of water to a boil in a large saucepan or pot, add 1 tablespoon of salt and drop in the pasta all at once, stirring well.
7 When the pasta is cooked *al dente*, drain it and toss it with the sauce, the remaining butter, and the grated cheese. Serve at once.

Also good with: *penne rigate, elicoidali, millerighe*

TONNARELLI AL RADICCHIO E BELGA

Tonnarelli with Radicchio and Belgian Endive

Vegetable oil is used here to prevent the butter from burning. When olive oil is used in other recipes, it is because its flavor enhances the dish.

INGREDIENTS

For *tonnarelli* made with 3 eggs (see page 36) *or* 1lb dried, store-bought egg *tonnarelli*

1 Tb vegetable oil
2 Tbs butter
⅓ cup finely chopped yellow onion
4oz bacon, cut into thin strips
from a ½ in thick slice
1lb radicchio, shredded
1lb Belgian endive, shredded
salt and freshly ground black pepper
1 cup heavy cream
1 Tbs finely chopped flat-leaf parsley
½ cup freshly grated parmigiano-reggiano *cheese*

PREPARATION

1 Put the vegetable oil, butter, and onion in a skillet (large enough to hold the *radicchio* and endive later) over a medium heat until the onion has softened and turned a rich golden color.
2 Add the bacon and cook until it is well browned but not crisp.
3 Add the *radicchio* and endive, season with salt and black pepper and stir until the vegetables are coated with the oil and butter. Turn the heat down to low, cover the skillet and cook, stirring occasionally, until the *radicchio* and endive have wilted completely and are almost creamy in consistency: about 15–20 minutes.
4 Pour 4 quarts of water into a large saucepan or pot and place over a high heat.
5 Uncover the skillet, raise the heat to medium-high and let any liquid the vegetables have given off evaporate. Pour in the cream and cook, stirring frequently, until it has reduced by half. Stir in the parsley and remove the skillet from the heat.
6 When the water for the pasta is boiling, and the sauce is off the heat, add 1 tablespoon of salt to the boiling water and put in the pasta all at once, stirring well.
7 When the pasta is cooked *al dente*, return the skillet with the sauce to a low heat, drain the pasta and toss it with the sauce in the skillet, adding the grated cheese. Serve at once.

Also good with: *spaghetti, fusilli lunghi, penne*

TONNARELLI AI GAMBERI E FUNGHI

Tonnarelli with Shrimp and Mushrooms

This sauce was inspired by a pasta dish Del Pearl, one of my sous-chefs, created. Shrimp and mushrooms are wonderful together, particularly with the addition of dried porcini.

INGREDIENTS

For *tonnarelli* made with 3 eggs (see page 36) *or* 1lb dried, store-bought egg *tonnarelli*

1oz dried porcini
⅓ cup extra-virgin olive oil
¾ cup yellow onion, thinly sliced lengthwise
¾lb cremini or fresh white mushrooms, thinly sliced
salt and freshly ground black pepper
½lb fresh ripe plum tomatoes, peeled, seeded and cut into ½in dice
¾lb medium shrimp, peeled, deveined if necessary, and cut into thirds
½ cup heavy cream

PREPARATION

1 Soak the dried *porcini* in a bowl with 1 cup lukewarm water for at least 20 minutes. Lift them out, squeezing the excess water back into the bowl, then rinse under cold running water and coarsely chop them. Filter the water the porcini soaked in through a paper towel or a coffee filter and set aside.

2 Put the olive oil and onion in a large skillet over a medium heat and cook until the onion softens and turns a rich golden color.

3 Add the reconstituted *porcini* with their filtered water, raise the heat to medium-high and cook, stirring, until almost all the water has evaporated. Add the fresh mushrooms, season with salt and black pepper and cook, stirring, until they are tender and the water they release has evaporated.

4 Pour 4 quarts of water into a large saucepan or pot and place over a high heat.

5 Add the tomatoes to the skillet and cook for 2 minutes. Stir in the shrimp, add the cream and cook, stirring frequently, until the cream has reduced by half. Remove the skillet from the heat.

6 When the water for the pasta is boiling, and the sauce is off the heat, add 1 tablespoon of salt to the boiling water and drop in the pasta all at once, stirring well.

7 When the pasta is cooked *al dente*, drain it and toss it with the sauce. Serve at once.

Also good with: *spaghetti, fusilli lunghi*

Porcini

Extra-virgin olive oil

Onion

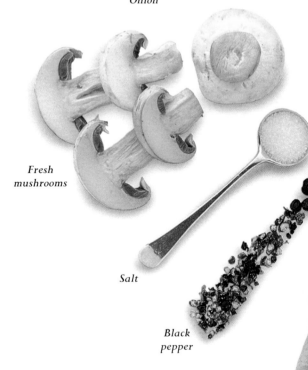

Fresh mushrooms

Salt

Black pepper

Tonnarelli ai
gamberi e funghi

Plum tomatoes

Shrimp

Heavy cream

Tonnarelli

105

TONNARELLI AL SUGO DI CIPOLLE

Tonnarelli with Onions, Anchovies, and Capers

The lowly onion becomes a succulent sauce with the help of slow cooking. The anchovies are only barely detectable.

INGREDIENTS

For *tonnarelli* made with 3 eggs (see page 36) or 1lb dried, store-bought egg *tonnarelli*

½ cup extra-virgin olive oil
6–8 anchovy fillets, chopped
4 cups yellow onions, finely chopped
salt and freshly ground black pepper
¼ cup dry white wine
3 Tbs capers
2 Tbs finely chopped parsley

PREPARATION

1 Put the olive oil and anchovies in a large skillet over a medium-low heat and stir with a wooden spoon until the anchovies have dissolved.
2 Add the onions, season lightly with salt and with black pepper and cook until the onions soften and become very tender: about 20–30 minutes.
3 Pour 4 quarts of water into a large saucepan or pot and place over a high heat.
4 Raise the heat under the skillet to medium-high and cook, stirring, until the onions become a rich, golden color.
5 Pour in the wine and cook until most of it has evaporated. Add the capers and parsley; cook for 2 more minutes. Remove the skillet from the heat.
6 When the water for the pasta is boiling, and the sauce is off the heat, add 1 tablespoon of salt to the boiling water and drop in the pasta all at once, stirring well.
7 When the pasta is cooked *al dente*, drain it and toss it with the sauce. Serve at once.

Also good with: *spaghetti, spaghettini, fusilli lunghi*

TONNARELLI AL MELONE

Tonnarelli with Cantaloupe

Although pasta with melon may sound an unlikely combination, I think you'll find the result surprisingly good. This is a recipe my parents and I discovered at a restaurant in Venice owned by a talented, creative, and very young chef called Silvano. What follows is a variation of my mother's recipe, which she based on the recipe Silvano gave her.

INGREDIENTS

For *tonnarelli* made with 3 eggs (see page 36) or 1lb dried, store-bought egg *tonnarelli*

4 Tbs (½ stick) butter
1 medium-sized cantaloupe, rind and seeds removed and flesh cut into ¼in dice
salt and freshly ground black pepper
1 Tb freshly squeezed lemon juice
1 tsp tomato paste
1 cup heavy cream
½ cup freshly grated parmigiano-reggiano cheese

PREPARATION

1 Pour 4 quarts of water into a large saucepan or pot and place over a high heat.
2 Melt the butter in a large skillet over a medium-high heat. When the butter foam subsides, stir in the cantaloupe, coating it well, and cook, stirring occasionally, until almost all the liquid it releases has evaporated.
3 Season generously with salt and black pepper and add the lemon juice and tomato paste. Pour in the cream and cook, stirring frequently, until it has reduced by half. Remove from the heat.
4 When the water for the pasta is boiling, and the sauce is off the heat, add 1 tablespoon of salt to the boiling water and drop in the pasta all at once, stirring well.
5 When the pasta is cooked *al dente*, drain it and toss it with the sauce, adding the grated cheese. Serve at once.

Also good with: *spaghetti* (but reduce the cream to ¾ cup)

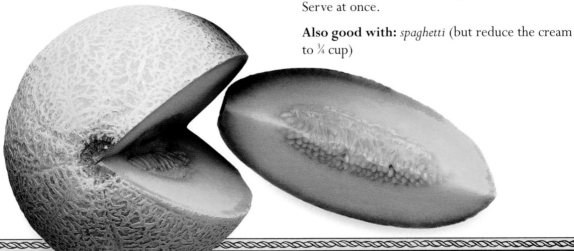

TONNARELLI AL GRANCHIO E RUCOLA

Tonnarelli with Crab and Arugula

This is a recipe I found in Positano in southern Italy, which I tried at home with great success using Dungeness crab, native to the Pacific coast of North America. Other types of crab, if meaty and sweet-tasting, work well too.

INGREDIENTS

For *tonnarelli* made with 3 eggs (see page 36)
or 1lb dried, store-bought egg *tonnarelli*

½ cup extra-virgin olive oil
1 tsp finely chopped garlic
¼ tsp (or to taste) red pepper flakes
1lb fresh ripe plum tomatoes, peeled, seeded
and cut into ½in dice
2 cups arugula, washed, long stems removed,
and coarsely shredded
salt
½ lb cooked crab meat

PREPARATION

1 Pour 4 quarts of water into a large saucepan or pot and place over a high heat.
2 Put the olive oil, garlic, and red pepper flakes in a large skillet over a medium-high heat and cook until the garlic begins to change color.
3 Add the tomatoes and cook for about 5 minutes until they begin to break down and the oil takes on a reddish color. This should happen quickly and the tomatoes should not go through the usual process of releasing water and cooking down until they have reduced. You may need to turn the heat up even higher but take care not to burn them.
4 Add the arugula, season with salt and add about 2 tablespoons of water. Cook until the arugula has wilted completely: 2 – 3 minutes.
5 When the water for the pasta is boiling, add 1 tablespoon of salt and drop in the pasta all at once, stirring well.
6 Add the crab to the sauce and cook, stirring for about 1 minute. Remove the skillet from the heat.
7 When the pasta is cooked *al dente*, drain it and toss it with the sauce. If it appears to be too dry, drizzle with a little fresh olive oil. Serve at once.

Also good with: *spaghetti, fusilli lunghi*

TONNARELLI AI CANESTRELLI

Tonnarelli with Scallops

This is one of my favorites of my mother's recipes, and this version has only slight variations from hers. Its preparation takes very little time and is a perfect example of the simple and direct Italian approach to bringing out the flavor of the main ingredient. The bread crumbs add texture and absorb some of the olive oil to help it cling to the pasta.

INGREDIENTS

For *tonnarelli* made with 3 eggs (see page 36)
or 1lb dried, store-bought egg *tonnarelli*

½ cup plus 2 Tbs extra-virgin olive oil
2 tsps finely chopped garlic
¼ tsp (or to taste) red pepper flakes
2 Tbs finely chopped flat-leaf parsley
1lb bay scallops, of which ¼ are finely chopped
salt
¼ cup plain bread crumbs, toasted

PREPARATION

1 Pour 4 quarts of water into a large saucepan or pot and place over a high heat.
2 Put ½ cup of the olive oil and all the garlic and red pepper flakes in a skillet over a medium-high heat and cook until the garlic begins to change color.
3 Add the parsley and stir well. Add the whole scallops, season with salt and cook, stirring, until they are no longer translucent: 3 – 5 minutes. Add the chopped scallops and cook, stirring, for another minute. Remove the skillet from the heat.
4 When the water for the pasta is boiling, and the sauce is off the heat, add 1 tablespoon of salt to the boiling water and drop in the pasta all at once, stirring well.
5 When the pasta is cooked *al dente*, drain it and toss it with the sauce, the toasted bread crumbs and the remaining 2 tablespoons of olive oil. Taste for salt and spiciness and serve at once.

Also good with: *spaghettini, spaghetti* (but for each one use only ⅓ cup of olive oil in step 2)

TUBI

Tubes

PENNE AL CAVOLFIORE E PANNA

Penne with Cauliflower, Tomatoes, and Cream

INGREDIENTS

For 1lb *penne*

¾lb cauliflower, leaves and stem removed
4 Tbs (½ stick) butter
⅓ cup finely chopped yellow onion
¼ tsp red pepper flakes
salt
1lb fresh ripe plum tomatoes, peeled, seeded
and cut into ½in dice
¾ cup heavy cream
½ cup freshly grated parmigiano-reggiano cheese

PREPARATION

1 Cook the cauliflower in abundant unsalted boiling water until tender. When cool enough to handle, cut it into ¾in pieces.

2 Pour 4 quarts of water into a large saucepan or pot and place over a high heat.

3 Melt the butter in a large skillet over a medium heat. Add the onion and cook until it has softened and turned a rich golden color.

4 Add the red pepper flakes and the cauliflower and season generously with salt. Sauté until the cauliflower is lightly browned: 8–10 minutes. Stir in the tomatoes and cook for 1 minute.

5 When the water for the pasta is boiling, add 1 tablespoon of salt and drop in the pasta all at once, stirring well.

6 Pour the cream into the skillet with the sauce and cook until the cream has reduced by half.

7 When the pasta is cooked *al dente*, drain it and toss it with the sauce, adding the grated cheese. Taste for salt and serve at once.

Also good with: *orecchiette, fusilli corti, gnocchi, lumache*

DENTI D'ELEFANTE AI PEPERONI E BIETE

Denti d'Elefante with Bell Peppers and Swiss Chard

INGREDIENTS

For 1lb *denti d'elefante*

3 Tbs extra-virgin olive oil
4 whole garlic cloves, lightly crushed and peeled
2 red bell peppers, cored and seeded, peeled, and cut into ¾ in squares
½ lb Swiss chard leaves, roughly chopped
salt and freshly ground black pepper
2 Tbs butter
2 Tbs balsamic vinegar
⅓ cup freshly grated parmigiano-reggiano *cheese*

PREPARATION

1 Put the olive oil and garlic in a large skillet over a high heat and cook until the garlic cloves have browned on all sides.
2 Discard the garlic. Add the bell peppers and cook them, stirring often, until they are lightly browned.
3 Reduce the heat to medium and add the chard and 2 tablespoons of water. Season with salt and black pepper and cook until the vegetables are tender. Remove the skillet from the heat.
4 Meanwhile, bring 4 quarts of water to a boil in a large saucepan or pot, add 1 tablespoon of salt, and drop in the pasta all at once, stirring well.
5 When the pasta is almost done, return the sauce to a low heat and swirl in the butter. Once the pasta is cooked *al dente*, drain it and toss it with the sauce in the skillet, adding the balsamic vinegar and the grated cheese. Serve at once.

Also good with: *fusilli corti, penne*

CAVATAPPI ALLA BOSCAIOLA

Cavatappi with Wild Mushrooms and Tomatoes

Boscaiola means "woodsman style" and this dish will evoke sensations of strolling through woods in autumn. If you have fresh porcini (Boletus edulis), *use them instead of the dried* porcini, *and disregard steps 1 and 3. In the absence of fresh* porcini, *dried* porcini *will endow cultivated mushrooms with the flavor of wild ones.*

INGREDIENTS

For 1lb *cavatappi*

1oz dried porcini
¼ *cup extra-virgin olive oil*
1 tsp finely chopped garlic
1 Tb finely chopped flat-leaf parsley
¾*lb cremini or fresh white mushrooms,*
cut into ½*in dice*
1 cup canned whole peeled tomatoes, with
their juice, coarsely chopped
salt and freshly ground black pepper
2 Tbs butter
⅓ *cup freshly grated* parmigiano-reggiano *cheese*

PREPARATION

1 Soak the dried *porcini* in a bowl with 1 cup lukewarm water for at least 20 minutes. Lift them out, squeezing the excess water back into the bowl, then rinse under cold running water and coarsely chop them. Filter the water they soaked in through a paper towel or a coffee filter and set aside.
2 Put the olive oil and garlic in a large skillet over a medium-high heat and cook until the garlic begins to change color, then stir in the parsley.
3 Add the reconstituted *porcini* with their filtered water and cook until the water has evaporated.
4 Put in the fresh mushrooms and cook until all the water they release has evaporated.
5 Add the tomatoes, season with salt and black pepper, and cook until the tomatoes have reduced and separated from the oil. Remove the skillet from the heat.

You can prepare the sauce ahead of time up to this point and refrigerate it.

6 Bring 4 quarts of water to a boil in a large saucepan or pot, add 1 tablespoon of salt, and drop in the pasta all at once, stirring well.
7 When the pasta is almost done, return the sauce to a medium-low heat. Once the pasta is cooked *al dente*, drain it and toss it with the sauce, adding the butter and the grated cheese. Serve at once.

Also good with: *maccheroni, fusilli lunghi, penne*

Flat-leaf parsley

Garlic

Extra-virgin olive oil

Porcini

Fresh
mushrooms

Canned
tomatoes

Salt

Black
pepper

Butter

Parmigiano-
reggiano

Cavatappi

**Cavatappi
alla boscaiola**

ELICOIDALI AL POLLO

Elicoidali with Braised Chicken and Tomatoes

I have never been particularly fond of chicken with pasta because I have always found the chicken too bland in flavor and texture. However, customers often requested a chicken sauce. I wanted to create a good one, and I discussed the dilemma with my mother. She suggested braising a chicken with tomatoes, then removing the meat from the bone and returning it to cook in the tomato and its own juices until it became a sauce. I tried it and, with the addition of a small amount of red pepper flakes, came up with a dish that proved successful and popular.

INGREDIENTS

For 1lb *elicoidali*

3 Tbs butter
2 Tbs vegetable oil
6 whole garlic cloves, lightly crushed and peeled
2 sprigs fresh rosemary **or** 1 tsp finely chopped dried
2lbs chicken legs, thighs and wings
½ cup dry white wine
2 cups canned whole peeled tomatoes, with
their juice, coarsely chopped
¼ tsp red pepper flakes
salt
⅓ cup freshly grated parmigiano-reggiano cheese

PREPARATION

1 Put 1 tablespoon of the butter and all the vegetable oil, garlic, and rosemary in a casserole (large enough to hold the chicken pieces without too much overlap) over a medium-high heat. Cook until the garlic cloves have browned nicely.
2 Discard the garlic. Put in the chicken pieces, skin-side down. Brown on all sides, transferring to a plate when done (it will be easier if you do not crowd the pan so, if necessary, cook the chicken in two batches).
3 Discard the rosemary (if using fresh sprigs) and return all the chicken to the pan. Raise the heat to high, pour in the white wine and let it bubble for about 1 minute so that the alcohol evaporates.

4 Add the tomatoes and the red pepper flakes and season with salt. When the tomatoes start to bubble, turn the heat down to low and cover the pan with the lid askew. Cook, turning the chicken occasionally and adding some water if more liquid is needed, until the meat is very tender and almost falls off the bone: 45 minutes to an hour. Cooking it a little longer will not hurt, nor should you worry if there seems to be a lot of liquid left over when the chicken is done.
5 Take out the chicken pieces and allow them to cool. When cool enough to handle, remove the meat from the bone in small pieces, discarding the fat and skin. Skim off the fat from the sauce and return the meat to it.

 You can prepare the sauce ahead of time up to this point and refrigerate it.

6 Bring 4 quarts of water to a boil in a large saucepan or pot, add 1 tablespoon of salt, and drop in the pasta all at once, stirring well.
7 Reheat the sauce over a medium-low heat. If the sauce was prepared ahead of time, the chicken may have absorbed all the liquid and become too dry. You can add a little chicken broth or water to moisten it. If, however, there is too much liquid, simply raise the heat and let it reduce down.
8 When the pasta is cooked *al dente*, drain it and toss it with the sauce, the remaining butter, and the grated cheese. Taste for salt and serve at once.

Also good with: *penne, rigatoni, lumache, pappardelle*

PENNE AI QUATTRO FORMAGGI

Penne with Four Cheeses

Pasta and cheese is an inspired combination with a wide appeal and almost everyone has their favorite concoction. This is mine. The pronounced taste of the gorgonzola, the richness of the fontina, the savor of the parmigiano-reggiano and the delicate creaminess of the mascarpone all complement each other perfectly, and when the dish is baked, the pasta absorbs all the flavors. Choose Italian-made cheeses.

INGREDIENTS

For 1lb *penne*

1 Tb butter
½ cup heavy cream
4oz fontina, *grated*
2oz gorgonzola, *crumbled*
2oz mascarpone
⅓ cup freshly grated parmigiano-reggiano *cheese*
salt and freshly ground black pepper

PREPARATION

1 Preheat the oven to 450°F.
2 Bring 4 quarts of water to a boil in a large saucepan or pot, add 1 tablespoon of salt, and drop in the pasta all at once, stirring well.
3 Put the butter and cream in a saucepan over a low heat. Stir until the butter has melted, then add all the cheeses, reserving 2 tablespoons of the grated *parmigiano-reggiano*. Stir constantly until the cheeses have melted into the cream, then season with salt and black pepper. Remove the pan from the heat and set aside.
4 When the pasta is *molto al dente* (about 1 minute away from being *al dente*), drain it and toss it with the sauce in a bowl until the pasta is well coated.
5 Transfer to individual bake-and-serve dishes, or a single ovenproof casserole large enough to accommodate the pasta to a depth of no more than about 1⅛in. Sprinkle the remaining 2 tablespoons of *parmigiano-reggiano* on top and bake until golden brown: about 10–15 minutes. When you take the dish out of the oven allow it to rest for 5 minutes before serving.

Fontina

Gorgonzola

Mascarpone

Parmigiano-reggiano

PASTA E FAGIOLI ASCIUTTA

Pasta with White Beans and Tomatoes

This is a dish I sampled in Naples. Asciutta refers to pasta with sauce, as opposed to soup, and this is similar to the classic pasta and bean soup except that it is prepared as a sauce. I like to serve it with cavatappi.

INGREDIENTS

For 1lb *cavatappi*

3 Tbs extra-virgin olive oil, plus
additional for serving
2 Tbs butter
4 Tbs finely chopped yellow onion
3 Tbs finely diced carrot
3 Tbs finely diced celery
4oz prosciutto, finely diced
1½ cups canned whole peeled tomatoes, with
their juice, coarsely chopped
salt and freshly ground black pepper
1 cup canned cranberry beans or white beans, drained
2 Tbs finely chopped flat-leaf parsley
⅓ cup freshly grated parmigiano-reggiano cheese

PREPARATION

1 Put the olive oil, butter, and onion in a saucepan over a medium heat and sauté until the onion softens and turns a rich golden color.
2 Stir in the carrot and celery and cook until they begin to brown lightly. Add the *prosciutto* and cook for about 2 minutes until it loses its raw color.
3 Add the tomatoes, season with salt and black pepper, and cook until they have reduced and separated from the oil: about 15–20 minutes.
4 Pour 4 quarts of water into a large saucepan or pot and place over a high heat.
5 Add the beans with ½ cup of water to the sauce and cook for 5 minutes. Take half of the beans out, process them through a food mill or mash them with a fork, and return to the pan.
6 When the water for the pasta is boiling, add 1 tablespoon of salt and drop in the pasta all at once, stirring well.
7 Add the parsley to the sauce and cook for 2–3 more minutes. The sauce should be liquid enough to pour out of a spoon but thick enough to coat it. If necessary add a little more water, or cook a little longer if it is too runny.
8 When the pasta is cooked *al dente*, drain it, and toss it with the sauce and the grated cheese. Grind fresh pepper and drizzle a tiny amount of high quality extra-virgin olive oil over each serving.

Also good with: *radiatori, lumache, conchiglie*

RIGATONI AL RAGU DI AGNELLO

Rigatoni with Lamb Ragù

A ragù is any sauce in which meat and vegetables, usually including tomatoes, are simmered together for a long time.

INGREDIENTS

For 1lb *rigatoni*

½oz dried porcini *mushrooms*
2 Tbs extra-virgin olive oil
3 Tbs butter
¼ cup finely chopped yellow onion
⅓ cup finely diced peeled carrot
⅓ cup finely diced celery
1 tsp fresh rosemary **or** ½ tsp dried, finely chopped
2 tsps juniper berries
¾lb boneless lamb, cut into ¼in dice
salt and freshly ground black pepper
⅓ cup dry white wine
1½ cups canned whole peeled tomatoes, with
their juice, coarsely chopped
¼ cup freshly grated parmigiano-reggiano cheese

PREPARATION

1 Soak the dried *porcini* in a bowl with 1 cup lukewarm water for at least 20 minutes. Lift them out, squeezing the excess water back into the bowl, then rinse under cold running water and coarsely chop them. Filter the water they soaked in through a paper towel or a coffee filter and set aside.
2 Put the olive oil, 1 tablespoon of the butter, and all the onion in a saucepan over a medium-low heat. When the onion has turned a rich golden color, add the carrot, celery, rosemary, and juniper berries. Continue sautéing until the vegetables are lightly browned.
3 Raise the heat to medium-high and put in the lamb. Cook, stirring, until the lamb has lost its raw color. Season with salt and black pepper and pour in the white wine.
4 Let the wine bubble until it has reduced by half, then add the reconstituted *porcini* and their filtered water, and the tomatoes. Once the sauce has come to a boil, turn the heat down to low and cook for a minimum of 2 hours, stirring occasionally. The sauce is done when it is no longer watery and the lamb is very tender. Remove from the heat and set aside.

 You can prepare the sauce ahead of time up to this point and refrigerate it.

5 Bring 4 quarts of water to a boil in a large saucepan or pot, add 1 tablespoon of salt, and drop in the pasta all at once, stirring well.
6 When the pasta is almost done, return the pan with the sauce to a medium heat. Once the pasta is cooked *al dente*, drain it and toss it with the sauce, adding the remaining butter and the grated cheese. Serve at once.

Also good with: *millerighe, elicoidali*

Rigatoni al ragù di agnello

SALSICCIA DI MAIALE

Homemade Pork Sausage

*The most common pork sausage used in Italy is mild and
not heavily spiced; it is the kind best suited to the
recipes in this book. I found it difficult to buy a
comparable sausage outside Italy, so I decided to try
making my own. Making sausage is really very simple,
and no special equipment is needed unless you use
casings. You can increase this recipe to make a
large batch and then freeze it in single-use portions.*

INGREDIENTS

1lb ground pork
1 tsp salt
1 tsp freshly ground black pepper
1 tsp fresh rosemary or ½ tsp dried, finely chopped
½ tsp finely chopped garlic
2 Tbs dry white wine

PREPARATION

1 Combine all the ingredients in a bowl and mix
thoroughly with your hands.
2 Cover with plastic wrap and refrigerate
overnight before using or freezing.

PENNE AI RAPINI E SALSICCIA

Penne with Broccoli Rabe and Sausage

*The savoriness of pork sausage and the slight bitterness
of rapini make a great combination. If you cannot find
rapini, try any strong-tasting greens, such as a
combination of curly endive and dandelion leaves.*

INGREDIENTS

For 1lb *penne*

*1½lbs broccoli rabe or other bitter greens (see
introductory note above)*
*½lb mild Italian pork sausage, crumbled, or
homemade pork sausage (see recipe above)*
⅓ cup extra-virgin olive oil
1 tsp finely chopped garlic
salt and freshly ground black pepper
2 Tbs butter
¼ cup freshly grated pecorino romano cheese

PREPARATION

1 Trim the stems of the *broccoli rabe* or other greens
and cook in salted boiling water until tender: about
5 minutes. Drain and, when cool enough to
handle, coarsely chop.
2 Pour 4 quarts of water into a large saucepan or
pot and place over a high heat.
3 Put the sausage and about ¼ cup of water in a
large skillet over a medium-high heat. As the
sausage cooks, break it up with a wooden spoon.
Once all the water has evaporated, let the sausage
brown a little, then add another tablespoon of
water and loosen any bits from the bottom of the
pan with the spoon.
4 When the water for the pasta is boiling, add
1 tablespoon of salt and drop in the pasta all at
once, stirring well.
5 Once all the water from the sauce has
evaporated, add the olive oil and the garlic. Sauté
until the garlic begins to change color, then add
the cooked greens and cook for 2–3 minutes.
Season with salt and black pepper (bearing in mind
that there is already salt and pepper in the sausage),
remove the skillet from the heat and set aside.
6 When the pasta is cooked *al dente*, drain it and
toss it with the sauce, adding the butter and the
grated cheese. Serve at once.

Also good with: *conchiglie, lumache, fusilli corti*

MACCHERONI ALLA SALSICCIA E RICOTTA

Maccheroni with Sausage, Tomatoes, and Ricotta

INGREDIENTS

For 1lb *maccheroni*

2 Tbs butter
½ cup finely chopped yellow onion
½ lb mild Italian pork sausage, crumbled,
or homemade pork sausage (see opposite)
1½ cups canned whole peeled tomatoes, with
their juice, coarsely chopped
salt and freshly ground black pepper
½ cup whole-milk ricotta
2 Tbs freshly torn basil leaves
¼ cup freshly grated parmigiano-reggiano *cheese*

PREPARATION

1 Melt the butter in a large skillet over a medium-high heat. Add the onion and cook until it softens and turns a rich golden color.
2 Add the sausage and break it up with a wooden spoon. Cook until the sausage has browned lightly.
3 Stir in the tomatoes, season lightly with salt and black pepper (bearing in mind that there will be salt and pepper in the sausage) and continue cooking until the tomatoes have reduced and separated from the butter and sausage fat. Remove the skillet from the heat and set aside.
4 Meanwhile, bring 4 quarts of water to a boil in a large saucepan or pot, add 1 tablespoon of salt, and drop in the pasta all at once, stirring well.
5 When the pasta is almost done, return the skillet with the sauce to a medium heat and add the *ricotta* and basil, mixing them in evenly.
6 When the pasta is cooked *al dente*, drain it and toss it with the sauce, adding the grated cheese. Serve at once.

Also good with: *penne, fusilli lunghi, fusilli corti, rigatoni, millerighe, elicoidali*

PENNE AL PROSCIUTTO E POMODORI SECCHI

Penne with Prosciutto, Sun-Dried Tomatoes, and Cream

Jim Foley, who has worked with me as sous-chef, created this simple, tasty dish.

INGREDIENTS

For 1lb *penne*

2 Tbs butter
⅓ cup finely chopped yellow onion
2oz prosciutto, *cut into thin strips*
from an ⅛in thick slice
2 Tbs coarsely chopped sun-dried tomatoes in oil
1 cup heavy cream
salt
¼ cup freshly grated parmigiano-reggiano *cheese*

PREPARATION

1 Pour 4 quarts of water into a large saucepan or pot and place over a high heat.
2 Melt the butter in a large skillet over a medium-high heat. Add the onion and cook until it softens and turns a rich golden color, then stir in the *prosciutto* and cook until it begins to brown.
3 When the water for the pasta is boiling, add 1 tablespoon of salt and drop in the pasta all at once, stirring well.
4 Meanwhile, add the sun-dried tomatoes and cream to the skillet with the onion and *prosciutto*, season lightly with salt and continue cooking until the cream has reduced by half. Remove the skillet from the heat and set aside.
5 When the pasta is cooked *al dente*, drain it and toss it with the sauce, adding the grated cheese. Taste for salt and serve at once.

Also good with: *farfalle, bucatini, garganelli*

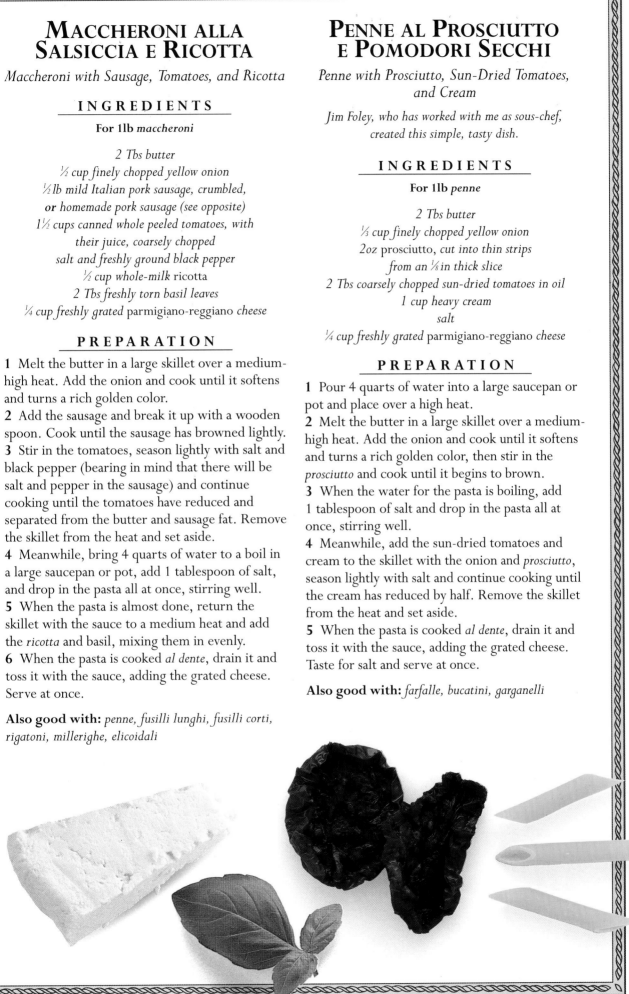

Farfalle al salmone
(page 121)

Fusilli corti alle zucchine
(page 120)

**Maccheroni alla
salsiccia e ricotta
(page 117)**

FORME SPECIALI
Special Shapes

FUSILLI CORTI ALLE ZUCCHINE

Fusilli with Zucchini

INGREDIENTS

For 1lb *fusilli*

⅓ cup extra-virgin olive oil
1 cup very thinly sliced yellow onion
1 tsp finely chopped garlic
1 Tb finely chopped flat-leaf parsley
1 lb zucchini, trimmed and cut into sticks 1½ in long
and ¼ in wide
2 Tbs shredded fresh basil
1 tsp finely chopped fresh mint
salt and freshly ground black pepper
¼ cup freshly grated pecorino romano *cheese*

PREPARATION

1 Put the olive oil and onion in a large skillet over a medium-low heat. Cook, stirring occasionally, until the onion has softened and turned a rich golden color.
2 Pour 4 quarts of water into a large saucepan or pot and place over a high heat.
3 Raise the heat under the skillet to medium-high and add the garlic. Cook, stirring frequently, for about 1 minute, then add the parsley and the zucchini and stir well. Cook, stirring occasionally, until the zucchini are tender and lightly browned: 5 – 10 minutes.
4 Stir in the basil and the mint and season with salt and black pepper. Remove the pan from the heat and set aside.
5 When the water for the pasta is boiling, add 1 tablespoon of salt and drop in the pasta all at once, stirring well.
6 When the pasta is cooked *al dente*, drain it and toss it with the sauce, adding the grated cheese. Serve at once.

Also good with: *fusilli lunghi, eliche*

ORECCHIETTE AL CAVOLFIORE

Orecchiette with Cauliflower and Pancetta

INGREDIENTS

For 1lb *orecchiette*

1 lb cauliflower, leaves and stem removed
¼ cup extra-virgin olive oil
1 tsp finely chopped garlic
3oz pancetta, cut into thin strips from a ¼ in thick slice
salt and freshly ground black pepper
¼ cup freshly grated pecorino romano *cheese*

PREPARATION

1 Cook the cauliflower in abundant unsalted boiling water for 6 – 8 minutes or until tender. When cool enough to handle, cut it into ½ in pieces.
2 Pour 4 quarts of water into a large saucepan or pot and place over a high heat.
3 Put the olive oil and garlic in a large skillet over a medium-high heat. When the garlic begins to sizzle, add the *pancetta* and sauté until it is browned but not crisp.
4 Turn the heat down to medium and stir in the cauliflower. Season with salt and black pepper and cook, stirring occasionally, until the cauliflower is lightly browned: 8 – 10 minutes. Remove the skillet from the heat and set aside.
5 When the water for the pasta is boiling, add 1 tablespoon of salt and drop in the pasta all at once, stirring well.
6 When the pasta is cooked *al dente*, drain it and toss it with the sauce, adding the grated cheese. Serve at once.

Also good with: *fusilli corti, strozzapreti*

FARFALLE AL SALMONE

Bow Tie Pasta with Fresh Salmon

Salmon is not commonly used in Italy but where I live in the Pacific Northwest of the US, fresh salmon is abundant and very good. To take advantage of this popular fish I devised the following recipe, which has had great success whenever I've served it.

INGREDIENTS

For 1lb *farfalle*

¼ cup extra-virgin olive oil
1 tsp finely chopped garlic
¼ tsp red pepper flakes
2 cups canned whole peeled tomatoes, with their juice, coarsely chopped
salt
½ lb fresh boned salmon, cut into ½ in dice
1 cup heavy cream
2 Tbs shredded fresh basil

PREPARATION

1 Put the olive oil, garlic and red pepper flakes in a large skillet over a medium-high heat and cook until the garlic begins to change color.
2 Add the tomatoes and season with salt. When the tomatoes begin to bubble, turn the heat down to medium-low and cook until the tomatoes have reduced and separated from the oil: about 20 minutes. Remove from the heat and set aside.

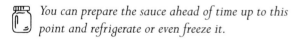 *You can prepare the sauce ahead of time up to this point and refrigerate or even freeze it.*

3 Bring 4 quarts of water to a boil in a large saucepan or pot, add 1 tablespoon of salt, and drop in the pasta all at once, stirring well.
4 Return the skillet with the tomato sauce to a medium-high heat and add the salmon, cream, and a pinch of salt. Cook over a medium-high heat until the cream has reduced by half. Stir in the basil and remove from the heat.
5 When the pasta is cooked *al dente*, drain it and toss it with the sauce. Taste for salt and spiciness and serve at once.

Also good with: *penne*

FARFALLE AL SALMONE AFFUMICATO

Bow Tie Pasta with Smoked Salmon and Roasted Bell Peppers

You need a smoked fish that you can flake for this recipe. If you cannot get thick, flakeable fillets of smoked salmon, use smoked trout fillets instead. Don't use lox.

INGREDIENTS

For 1lb *farfalle*

2 red bell peppers
2 garlic cloves, peeled
½ lb flakeable smoked salmon **or** trout fillet
(see introductory note above)
1 cup heavy cream
salt and freshly ground black pepper
2 Tbs shredded fresh basil

PREPARATION

1 Roast the peppers under the broiler or over an open flame until the skin is charred on all sides. Place them in a bowl and cover the bowl tightly with plastic wrap. After about 20 minutes take the peppers out, cut them in half, remove the core, and scrape away the blistered skin and the seeds. Place the peppers and the garlic in a food processor or blender and grind until creamy. Remove and set aside.
2 Bring 4 quarts of water to a boil in a large saucepan or pot, add 1 tablespoon of salt, and drop in the pasta all at once, stirring well.
3 Flake the smoked fish with a fork. Put the fish, the pepper purée, and the cream in a large skillet over a medium-high heat. Season with salt (remembering that the fish is already salty) and black pepper and cook until the cream has reduced by half. Stir in the basil and remove from the heat.
4 When the pasta is cooked *al dente*, drain it and toss it with the sauce. Taste for salt and pepper and serve at once.

Also good with: *penne, fusilli corti, conchiglie*

FUSILLI CORTI ALLA CAMPAGNOLA

Fusilli with Eggplant, Zucchini, and Bell Peppers

INGREDIENTS

For 1lb *fusilli*

½ cup extra-virgin olive oil
¾ cup thinly sliced yellow onion
1 tsp finely chopped garlic
1 cup peeled and diced eggplant
1 cup diced zucchini
1 red bell pepper **or** ½ a red and ½ a yellow bell pepper,
cored and seeded, peeled and cut into 1in squares
salt
pinch of red pepper flakes
½ lb fresh ripe plum tomatoes, peeled, seeded and
cut into ½in dice, **or** ½ cup canned whole peeled
tomatoes, with their juice, coarsely chopped

PREPARATION

1 Put the olive oil and onion in a large skillet
over a medium heat and cook until the onion has
softened and turned a rich golden color.
2 Stir in the garlic, cook for 1 minute, then add
the eggplant (do not worry if the eggplant soaks
up all the oil, it will release it once it is cooked).
Cover the skillet and cook for about 5 minutes.
3 Pour 4 quarts of water into a large saucepan or
pot and place over a high heat.
4 Uncover the skillet and add the zucchini and
bell peppers to the eggplant. Season with salt and
add the red pepper flakes. Cook, stirring
frequently, until the vegetables start to become
tender: about 5 minutes.
5 When the water for the pasta is boiling, add
1 tablespoon of salt and drop in the pasta all at
once, stirring well.
6 Meanwhile, add the tomatoes to the sauce and
continue cooking until they have reduced and
separated from the oil: about 5 minutes. Remove
the skillet from the heat and set aside.
7 When the pasta is cooked *al dente*, drain it and
toss it thoroughly with the sauce. Taste for salt and
serve at once.

Also good with: *penne rigate, rigatoni, elicoidali,
millerighe, fusilli lunghi*

Zucchini

Eggplant

Garlic

Onion

Extra-virgin olive oil

Red bell pepper

Yellow bell pepper

Salt

Red pepper flakes

Plum tomatoes

Fusilli

Fusilli corti alla campagnola

RUOTE DI CARRO CON PEPERONATA

Cartwheels with Bell Peppers and Onions

INGREDIENTS

For 1lb *ruote di carro*

⅓ cup extra-virgin olive oil
2 cups thinly sliced yellow onion
2 red and 2 yellow bell peppers, cored and seeded,
peeled and cut lengthwise into strips ¼ in wide
1 cup canned whole peeled tomatoes, with
their juice, coarsely chopped
salt and freshly ground black pepper
pinch of red pepper flakes
1 Tb finely chopped flat-leaf parsley

PREPARATION

1 Put the olive oil and onion in a large skillet over a low heat. Cook, stirring occasionally, until the onion has wilted and turned golden in color.

2 Turn the heat up to medium, add the bell peppers and cook, stirring frequently, until they soften slightly: about 2–3 minutes.
3 Stir in the tomatoes, season with salt and black pepper and add the crushed red pepper flakes. Stir well and cook until the tomatoes have reduced and separated from the oil: about 20 minutes.
4 Add the parsley, stir for about 30 seconds, and remove from the heat. Set aside.

You can prepare the sauce ahead of time up to this point and refrigerate it.

5 Bring 4 quarts of water to a boil in a large saucepan or pot, add 1 tablespoon of salt, and drop in the pasta all at once, stirring well.
6 When the pasta is almost done, return the skillet with the sauce to a medium heat.
7 Once the pasta is cooked *al dente*, drain it and toss it with the sauce. Taste for salt and serve at once.

Also good with: *rigatoni, penne rigate, fusilli lunghi, fusilli corti*

CONCHIGLIE ALLA SALSICCIA E PANNA

Shells with Sausages, Tomatoes, and Cream

INGREDIENTS

For 1lb *conchiglie*

½ lb mild Italian pork sausages
2 Tbs butter
1 tsp fresh rosemary **or** ½ tsp dried, finely chopped
1½ lbs fresh ripe plum tomatoes, peeled,
seeded and cut into ½ in dice
pinch of red pepper flakes
salt
½ cup heavy cream
1 Tb finely chopped flat-leaf parsley
¼ cup freshly grated parmigiano-reggiano cheese

PREPARATION

1 Boil the sausages in water for 2–3 minutes. When they are cool enough to handle, slice them into thin rounds.

2 Pour 4 quarts of water into a large saucepan or pot and place over a high heat.

3 Melt the butter in a large skillet over a medium-high heat. Add the sausage and cook until it is lightly browned.

4 Add the rosemary, tomatoes, and 2 tablespoons of water. Cook until the water has evaporated and the tomatoes have just started to break down and form a sauce: about 5 minutes.

5 When the water for the pasta is boiling, add 1 tablespoon of salt and drop in the pasta all at once, stirring well.

6 Add the red pepper flakes to the sauce in the skillet and season lightly with salt (bearing in mind that there will be salt in the sausage). Pour in the cream and add the parsley. Cook, stirring frequently, until the cream has reduced by half. Remove the skillet from the heat and set aside.

7 When the pasta is cooked *al dente*, drain it and toss it with the sauce in the skillet, adding the grated cheese. Taste for salt and spiciness and serve at once.

LUMACHE AI CARCIOFI

Lumache with Artichokes, Pancetta, and Thyme

INGREDIENTS

For 1lb *lumache*

2 large artichokes
2 Tbs lemon juice
4 Tbs (½ stick) butter
½ cup finely chopped yellow onion
4oz pancetta, *cut into thin strips from a ½ in thick slice*
salt and freshly ground black pepper
½ tsp chopped fresh thyme **or** *¼ tsp dried*
⅓ cup freshly grated parmigiano-reggiano *cheese*

PREPARATION

1 Trim the artichokes as shown, slice them thinly and place in a bowl with cold water and the lemon juice to prevent them from becoming brown.
2 Melt the butter in a large skillet over a medium heat. Add the onion and cook until it softens and turns a rich golden color. Add the *pancetta* and continue sautéing until the *pancetta* is nicely browned but not crisp.
3 Pour 4 quarts of water into a large saucepan or pot and place over a high heat.
4 Drain the artichoke slices, rinse them under cold water and add to the skillet. Season with salt and black pepper and sprinkle with thyme, then stir a couple of times to coat them. Pour in enough water to come ½ in up the side of the skillet and cook uncovered until the artichokes are very tender: 10–15 minutes. You may need to add more water periodically. When done, remove from the heat and set aside.
5 When the water for the pasta is boiling, add 1 tablespoon of salt and drop in the pasta all at once, stirring well.
6 Once the pasta is almost done, return the sauce to the heat and boil away any excess liquid, leaving just a little moisture.
7 When the pasta is cooked *al dente*, drain it and toss it with the sauce, adding the grated cheese. Taste for salt and pepper and serve at once.

Also good with: *gnocchi, fusilli corti, fusilli lunghi, cavatappi, radiatori*

TRIMMING ARTICHOKES

1 *Remove the leaves of each artichoke by bending them back until they snap and pulling them down. The fresher the artichokes, the more easily the leaves will snap.*

2 Use a sharp knife to slice off the top. Discard it.

3 Scrape away the fuzzy choke from within the vegetable using a round knife such as a table knife.

4 Using a sharp paring knife, trim away all the dark green parts. Finally, cut off the stem, and the artichoke is ready for use.

**Lumache
ai carciofi**

STROZZAPRETI AI PORCINI E PEPERONI

Strozzapreti with Porcini and Bell Peppers

This is a recipe I found in a restaurant called Antonio Colonna in the tiny town of Labico outside Rome. The door to the restaurant has no sign and looks more like the entrance to a private home than to a restaurant. You ring the bell and are shown in to an elegant high-ceilinged room with six tables. There is no menu and you are served a spectacular seven-course meal selected for that day by the chef. This dish was the pasta course on the day of our visit.

INGREDIENTS

For 1lb *strozzapreti*

½ lb fresh or thawed frozen porcini, *cut into ½ in dice,* **or** *1oz dried* porcini
⅓ cup extra-virgin olive oil
4 – 6 whole garlic cloves, lightly crushed and peeled
2 sprigs fresh sage **or** *1 tsp dried*
1 sprig fresh rosemary **or** *1 tsp dried*
1lb cremini or fresh white mushrooms, cut into ½ in dice
1 red and 1 yellow bell pepper, cored and seeded, peeled and cut into ¼ in dice
salt and freshly ground black pepper
2 Tbs butter
⅓ cup freshly grated parmigiano-reggiano *cheese*

PREPARATION

1 If you are using fresh or frozen *porcini*, start with step 2, and omit step 3. If you are using dried *porcini*, soak them in a bowl with 1 cup lukewarm water for at least 20 minutes. Lift them out, squeezing excess water back into the bowl, then rinse under cold running water and coarsely chop them. Filter the water they soaked in through a paper towel or a coffee filter and set aside.

2 Put the olive oil, garlic, sage, and rosemary in a large skillet over a medium-high heat and cook, stirring occasionally, until the garlic cloves have browned on all sides. Take the skillet off the heat. Discard the garlic, along with the fresh herbs. If you are using dried herbs, remove them by pouring the oil through a strainer.

3 Add the soaked *porcini* with their filtered water to the skillet. (Doing this off the heat prevents the water from spattering.) Return the skillet with the *porcini* to a medium-high heat and cook until all the water has evaporated.

4 Add the fresh mushrooms, raise the heat to high and sauté until the water they give off has also evaporated.

5 If using fresh or frozen *porcini*, add them now and cook over a medium-high heat for 2 – 3 minutes, stirring frequently.

6 Add the red and yellow bell peppers, season with salt and black pepper and continue to cook over a medium-high heat until they are tender: 5 – 10 minutes. Remove the skillet from the heat and set aside.

You can prepare the sauce several hours ahead of time up to this point but do not refrigerate it.

7 Bring 4 quarts of water to a boil in a large saucepan or pot, add 1 tablespoon of salt, and drop in the pasta all at once, stirring well.

8 When the pasta is almost done, return the sauce to a medium heat and stir in the butter.

9 When the pasta is cooked *al dente*, drain it and toss it with the sauce, adding the grated cheese. Serve at once.

Also good with: *penne*

INSALATA DI FUSILLI E PENNE

Polly's Pasta Salad

When my wife, Polly, had to make a dish for a special party she had been invited to, she created this delicious pasta salad.

INGREDIENTS

For ½lb *fusilli corti* and ½lb *penne*

2 red bell peppers
1 medium-sized eggplant
⅓ cup extra-virgin olive oil
⅓ cup artichoke hearts, preserved in oil, quartered
8 – 10 green olives, pitted and julienned
8 – 10 black olives, pitted and julienned
2 Tbs capers
1 avocado, peeled and cut into ½ in chunks
1 Tb red wine vinegar
salt

PREPARATION

1 Roast the bell peppers under the broiler or over an open flame until the skin is charred on all sides. Place in a bowl and cover the bowl tightly with plastic wrap. After about 20 minutes take the peppers out, cut them in half, remove the core, and scrape away the blistered skin and the seeds. Cut the flesh into ½ in squares.
2 Roast the eggplant whole in the same way as the peppers, but instead of covering it in a bowl leave it out on a plate. When it is cool enough to handle, cut off the top and peel away the skin. Cut it in half lengthwise, remove most of the seeds and cut the flesh into ¾ in chunks.
3 Bring 4 quarts of water to a boil in a large saucepan or pot, add 1 tablespoon of salt, and drop in both pastas, stirring well (if they are the same brand, they will take the same amount of time to cook).
4 When the pasta is *molto al dente* (about 30 seconds away from being *al dente*), drain and toss in a bowl with 2 tablespoons of the olive oil.
5 Add the peppers, eggplant, and the rest of the ingredients to the bowl, with the remainder of the olive oil and a sprinkling of salt. Toss well and set aside to cool completely before serving, but do not refrigerate.

ORECCHIETTE ALLA VERZA

Orecchiette with Anchovies and Savoy Cabbage

This recipe is also very good with broccoli: use 2 cups boiled chopped broccoli florets in place of 6 cups shredded cabbage. Don't cover the pan in step 3; turn the heat up to high instead, sauté the broccoli for 5 minutes only, and skip step 5.

INGREDIENTS

For 1lb *orecchiette*

½ cup extra-virgin olive oil
4 whole garlic cloves, lightly crushed and peeled
6 – 8 anchovy fillets, chopped
6 cups savoy cabbage, shredded
salt and freshly ground black pepper
2 Tbs butter
⅓ cup freshly grated parmigiano-reggiano cheese

PREPARATION

1 Put the olive oil and garlic in a large skillet over a medium-high heat and cook until the garlic cloves have browned on all sides.
2 Discard the garlic. Turn the heat down to low and, once the oil has cooled slightly, add the anchovies (otherwise you may fry them). Cook, stirring with a wooden spoon, until the anchovies have dissolved.
3 Stir in the savoy cabbage, season with salt and black pepper, and toss until the cabbage is well coated with the anchovy oil. Cover the skillet and cook, stirring occasionally, until the cabbage is very tender: 20 – 30 minutes.
4 Pour 4 quarts of water into a large saucepan or pot and place over a high heat.
5 Uncover the skillet and raise the heat to medium-high to evaporate any water from the sauce. Once the water has evaporated and the cabbage has colored lightly, remove the skillet from the heat and set aside.
6 When the water for the pasta is boiling, add 1 tablespoon of salt and drop in the pasta all at once, stirring well.
7 Once the pasta is almost done, return the sauce to a medium heat and stir in the butter.
8 When the pasta is cooked *al dente*, drain it and toss it with the sauce, adding the grated cheese. Serve at once.

Also good with: *fusilli corti, cavatappi, strozzapreti*

MINESTRE
Soups

BRODO DI CARNE

Homemade Meat Broth

A homemade Italian meat broth is delicate and light, made with a combination of raw meats and vegetables. Do not confuse it with stock, which is usually more intense and concentrated, and is made with oven-baked bones and vegetables.

INGREDIENTS

*5 lbs beef and veal, meat and bones
(you can also use chicken)
1 tsp salt
2 carrots, peeled
2 – 3 celery stalks
1 medium-sized yellow onion, peeled
1 fresh ripe plum tomato or 1 whole canned tomato
1 sprig flat-leaf parsley
1 Tb whole black peppercorns*

PREPARATION

1 Put all the ingredients in a large stockpot, pour in enough cold water to cover by 2in and place over a high heat.
2 When the water begins to boil, turn the heat down to very low and skim off the froth that has come to the surface. Cover the pot with the lid askew. Cook at a very gentle simmer for about 3 hours.
3 When the broth is done, pour it through a strainer and let it cool completely. It will keep in the refrigerator for 3 days. If you want to keep it for longer, it is best to freeze it. Pour the stock into ice-cube trays and, once it is frozen, store the cubes in plastic bags in the freezer.

MINESTRA DI PASTA E CECI

Pasta and Chickpea Soup

My mother's chickpea soup is perfect for a cold winter's evening and if you have canned chickpeas you can produce it in less than 45 minutes from start to finish. The addition of homemade maltagliati *makes it even more delectable.*

INGREDIENTS

*⅓ cup extra-virgin olive oil
4 whole garlic cloves, lightly crushed and peeled
2 tsps fresh rosemary or 1 tsp dried, finely chopped
⅔ cup canned whole peeled tomatoes, with
their juice, coarsely chopped
2 cups drained canned chickpeas
3 cups homemade meat broth (see left) or
1 beef bouillon cube dissolved in 3 cups water
salt and freshly ground black pepper
½ lb homemade* maltagliati *or any
small, tubular pasta
¼ cup freshly grated* parmigiano-reggiano *cheese*

PREPARATION

1 Put the olive oil and garlic in a large, heavy-bottomed stockpot over a medium-high heat and cook until the garlic has browned on all sides.
2 Discard the garlic, then stir the rosemary into the oil. Remove the pot briefly from the heat and add the tomatoes. Reduce the heat to medium-low, return the pot and cook until the tomatoes have reduced and separated from the oil: 15–20 minutes.
3 Add the chickpeas, season with salt and black pepper, and cook for another 2–3 minutes.
4 Pour in the broth, cover the pot, and cook for 15 minutes more.
5 Use a slotted spoon to scoop up about a quarter of the chickpeas and either purée them through a food mill or mash them with a fork. Return them to the soup and raise the heat to medium-high. When the soup begins to boil, drop in the pasta and cover the pot.
6 When the pasta is *al dente*, take the soup off the heat and stir in the grated cheese. Let the soup rest for a few minutes before serving.

PASTA E FAGIOLI

Pasta and Bean Soup

There are many variations on the classic pasta and bean soup in Italy and my favorite is the one made in the Emilia-Romagna region. The best bean to use is the cranberry bean which is sometimes available fresh in the spring and summer. Dried cranberry beans also work quite well provided they are soaked in water overnight, or you can use canned cranberry beans or red kidney beans. This recipe is the classic method of preparing this soup that I learned from my mother.

INGREDIENTS

¼ cup extra-virgin olive oil, plus
additional for serving with the finished soup
2 Tbs finely chopped yellow onion
3 Tbs finely diced peeled carrot
3 Tbs finely diced celery
3–4 pork ribs **or** 2 small pork chops
¾ cup canned whole peeled tomatoes,
with their juice, coarsely chopped
3 cups fresh, frozen, **or** canned cranberry or
red kidney beans, **or** 2 cups dried cranberry
beans soaked overnight (see note above)
4 cups homemade meat broth (see opposite) **or**
1 beef bouillon cube dissolved in 4 cups water
salt
½ lb homemade maltagliati or any small,
tubular pasta
¼ cup freshly grated parmigiano-reggiano cheese
freshly ground black pepper

PREPARATION

1 Put the olive oil and onion in a large, heavy-bottomed stockpot over a medium heat and sauté until the onion turns a rich golden color.
2 Stir in the carrot and celery and sauté for another 2 minutes. Add the pork and cook, stirring occasionally, for about 10 minutes.
3 Add the tomatoes, turn the heat down to low and simmer for about 10 minutes or, if you are using canned beans in the next step, until the tomatoes have reduced: about 25 minutes.
4 Add the beans, stir well and add the broth. Cover the pot and cook until the beans are tender: about 45 minutes for fresh or dried-and-soaked beans, 5 minutes for canned beans (which are already cooked).
5 Remove the pork (but don't discard it – it makes a great snack for the cook at this point!). Use a slotted spoon to scoop up about a quarter of the beans. Purée them through a food mill or mash them with a fork and return them to the pot.

Season with salt (it's important not to add salt until the beans are fully cooked or the skins will become tough).

 The soup may be prepared ahead of time up to this point and refrigerated.

6 Check the density of the soup. It should not be watery but it should have enough liquid for the pasta to cook in it. If necessary add a little more broth or water. Raise the heat to medium-high. When the soup begins to boil, drop in the pasta.
7 When the pasta is *al dente*, remove the soup from the heat and stir in the grated cheese. The soup is best if you allow it to rest for a few minutes before serving. Once it is ready to serve, ladle it into bowls and season each serving with black pepper and a light drizzle of fresh olive oil.

MINESTRINA DEI BAMBINI

Children's Soup with Pastina

In Italy this is traditionally a soup made for small children or for people who are convalescing and do not feel up to a regular meal. It is a comforting and revitalizing soup.

INGREDIENTS

5 cups homemade meat broth (see opposite) **or**
2 beef or chicken bouillon cubes dissolved in 5 cups water
6oz pastina (small pasta for soup)
2 Tbs butter
¼ cup freshly grated parmigiano-reggiano cheese

PREPARATION

1 Bring the broth to a boil. Drop in the *pastina* and cook it briefly until it is *al dente*. Remove the pan from the heat.
2 Stir in the butter and the grated cheese and serve at once.

MINESTRA DI PASTA E VERDURE ALLA ROMANA

Roman Soup with Pasta and Vegetables

*In an old Italian book on pasta I came across
mention of a Roman soup made with pasta and
"various lettuces." It sounded interesting so I decided
to try making it with Swiss chard, mustard greens, butter
lettuce, and savoy cabbage. The result was a wonderful,
elegant soup, which far exceeded my expectations.*

INGREDIENTS

2 Tbs butter
3 Tbs extra-virgin olive oil
¼ cup finely chopped yellow onion
2 Tbs finely diced pancetta
¼ cup finely diced peeled carrot
¼ cup finely diced celery
½ tsp fresh rosemary or ¼ tsp dried, finely chopped
1½ cups roughly chopped Swiss chard or
(if chard is unavailable) spinach leaves
1 cup roughly chopped mustard green leaves or kale
1½ cups roughly chopped butter lettuce leaves
2 cups finely shredded savoy cabbage leaves
salt and freshly ground black pepper
5 cups homemade meat broth (see page 130) or
1 beef bouillon cube dissolved in 5 cups water
6oz tubetti, ditali or, my favorite, cavatappi
¼ cup freshly grated parmigiano-reggiano *cheese*

PREPARATION

1 Put the butter, one third of the olive oil, and all
the onion in a large, heavy-bottomed stockpot over
a medium-low heat.
2 When the onion has softened and turned a rich
golden color, stir in the *pancetta* and continue
cooking until it is lightly browned but not crisp.
3 Add the carrot, celery, and rosemary and sauté
until they are lightly browned.
4 Drop in all the greens and season with salt and
black pepper. Once the leaves have wilted, continue
sautéing for 2 minutes more, then pour in the
broth. When the broth begins to boil, turn the heat
down to low and cover the pot. Cook for 1 hour.
5 Raise the heat to medium-high. When the soup
begins to boil again, drop in the pasta and cover the
pot. When the pasta is *al dente*, pour the soup into
bowls. Drizzle the remaining olive oil over each
serving and sprinkle each with the grated cheese.
Serve at once.

Spinach

Fresh rosemary

Celery

Carrot

Pancetta

Onion

Extra-virgin
olive oil

Butter

Kale

Lettuce

Savoy
cabbage

Salt

Black
pepper

Broth

Tubetti

Parmigiano-
reggiano

**Minestra
alla romana**

PASTA RIPIENA E AL FORNO
Stuffed and Baked Pasta

TORTELLONI DI BIETE

Tortelloni Filled with Swiss Chard

It is with these tortelloni *that my life-long love of pasta began. I prefer them with the simple butter and tomato sauce on page 52 but they are also wonderful with just butter and* parmigiano-reggiano *cheese. They are shown* di spinaci *(stuffed with spinach) on page 53.*

INGREDIENTS

THE TORTELLONI
2lbs Swiss chard (more if the stalks are large) or fresh spinach or 2 x 10oz packages frozen spinach, thawed
salt
4 Tbs butter
¼ cup finely chopped yellow onion
2oz finely chopped prosciutto
1 cup whole-milk ricotta
1 egg yolk
½ cup freshly grated parmigiano-reggiano *cheese*
⅛ tsp freshly grated nutmeg
pasta dough made with 2 eggs (see page 36)

THE SAUCE
Burro e pomodoro *sauce (see page 52), made in advance, or 6 Tbs (¾ stick) butter, cut into small pieces*
½ cup freshly grated parmigiano-reggiano *cheese*

PREPARATION

THE TORTELLONI
1 If using fresh chard or spinach leaves, remove the stalks or stems and wash the leaves in several changes of cold water. Place them in a pan over a medium-high heat with ½ teaspoon of salt and just the water that clings to them after washing. Cover and cook until the leaves are tender: about 8–12 minutes. If using frozen spinach, cook it for about 3 minutes in enough salted boiling water to cover.
2 Drain the leaves and, when cool enough to handle, squeeze out excess water, and chop.
3 Melt the butter in a skillet over a medium heat. Add the onion and cook until it turns a rich golden color. Add the *prosciutto* and sauté for 1 minute. Add the Swiss chard or spinach and cook, stirring, for 3 minutes (do not worry if it absorbs all the butter). Transfer to a bowl. Allow to cool.
4 Mix in the *ricotta*, egg yolk, grated cheese and nutmeg. Combine thoroughly, and taste for salt.

5 Roll out the pasta dough as thinly as possible and make the stuffed *tortelloni* as shown on page 42. Spread them out on a clean kitchen towel.
6 Bring 4 quarts of water to a boil in a large saucepan or pot, add 1 tablespoon each of salt and of olive oil, and slide in the pasta using the kitchen towel it was spread out on.
7 Gently reheat the *Burro e pomodoro* sauce, or melt the butter.
8 When the sealed edges of the *tortelloni* are cooked *al dente*, drain them and transfer to a serving dish. Pour the sauce or melted butter and sprinkle the grated cheese over them and gently toss until the pasta is evenly coated. Serve at once.

TORTELLINI ALLA PANNA

Tortellini with Cream

There is a story that tells of a pasta-maker secretly in love with a young girl who worked for him. Before she started work she would change her clothes in the back room, and one day the owner gave in to the temptation to peek through the keyhole. All he could see was her navel but he found it so beautiful that he picked up a small disk of pasta and mimicked its shape. This, so legend has it, is how the first tortellino *was born.*

INGREDIENTS

THE TORTELLINI
3 Tbs butter
1 Tb vegetable oil
2oz lean boneless pork loin,
cut into ½in cubes
salt and freshly ground black pepper
3oz boneless, skinless chicken breast, trimmed of all fat, and cut into ½in cubes
2oz very finely chopped mortadella
¾ cup whole-milk ricotta
1 egg yolk
¼ tsp freshly grated nutmeg
½ cup freshly grated parmigiano-reggiano *cheese*
pasta dough made with 2 eggs (see page 36)

THE SAUCE
2 Tbs butter
½ cup heavy cream
⅓ cup freshly grated parmigiano-reggiano *cheese*

PREPARATION

THE TORTELLINI

1 Put the butter, oil, and pork in a skillet over a medium heat. Season with salt and black pepper and cook, stirring, for 5 minutes. Remove the pork with a slotted spoon and set aside.

2 Add the chicken to the skillet, season with salt and black pepper, and cook, stirring, for 2–3 minutes. Remove the chicken with a slotted spoon and set aside together with the pork.

3 Chop the pork and chicken finely (but not to a paste) in a food processor or by hand. Transfer to a bowl and, using a fork, mix in the *mortadella*, *ricotta*, egg yolk, nutmeg, and grated cheese. Knead to amalgamate the ingredients thoroughly. Taste for salt and set aside.

4 Roll out the pasta dough as thinly as possible and make the stuffed *tortellini* as shown on page 42. Spread them out on a clean kitchen towel.

THE SAUCE

1 Pour 4 quarts of water into a large saucepan or pot and place over a high heat.

2 Melt the butter for the sauce in a large skillet over a medium-high heat. Pour in the cream and cook, stirring frequently, until the cream has reduced by half. Remove the pan from the heat and set aside.

3 When the water for the pasta is boiling, add 1 tablespoon each of salt and of olive oil, and slide in the pasta using the kitchen towel it was spread out on.

4 When the sealed edges of the *tortellini* are cooked *al dente*, return the skillet with the sauce to a low heat, drain the *tortellini* and toss very gently with the cream and butter sauce in the skillet, adding the grated cheese, a pinch of salt and some grindings of black pepper. Taste for seasoning and serve at once.

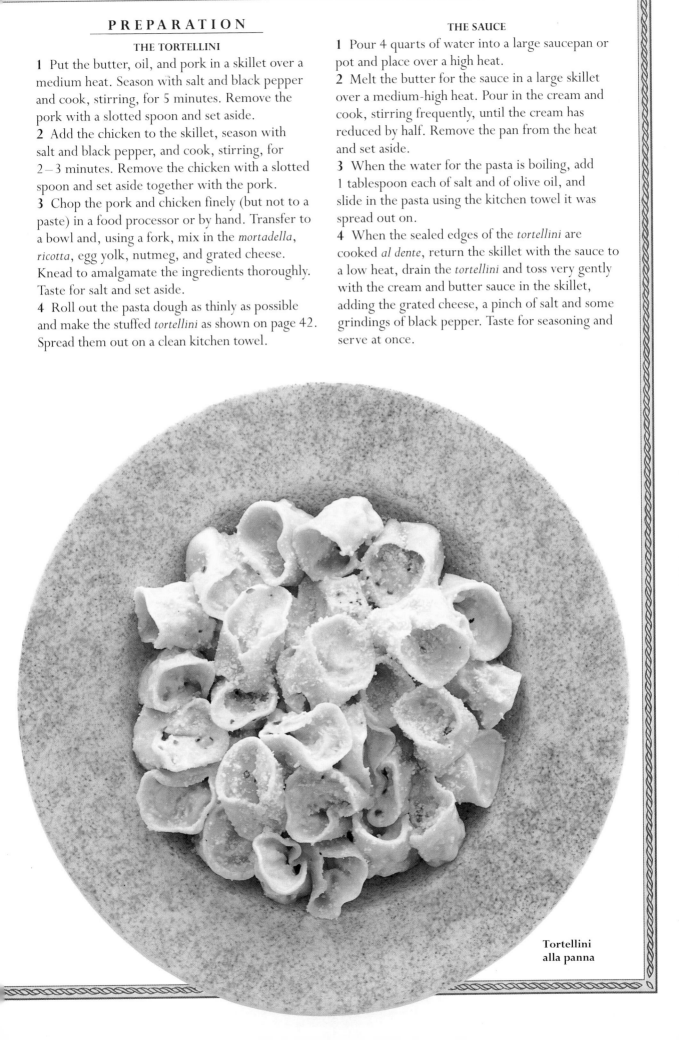

Tortellini alla panna

TORTELLONI DI RICOTTA E PREZZEMOLO

Tortelloni Filled with Ricotta and Parsley

These tortelloni are a speciality of Bologna. Unlike the pillow-shaped versions elsewhere in this section, Bolognese tortelloni are shaped like large cappelletti. The best sauce is the pink tomato sauce used in the recipe for Tortelloni di carciofi (page 138).

INGREDIENTS

1½ cups whole-milk ricotta
½ cup finely chopped flat-leaf parsley
1 egg yolk
⅛ tsp freshly grated nutmeg
1 cup freshly grated parmigiano-reggiano cheese
salt and freshly ground black pepper
pasta dough made with 2 eggs (see page 36)

PREPARATION

1 In a mixing bowl, use a fork to combine the *ricotta*, parsley, egg yolk, nutmeg and half of the grated cheese. Season with salt and black pepper.
2 Roll out the pasta dough as thinly as possible and make the stuffed *tortelloni* as shown on page 43. Spread them out on a clean kitchen towel.
3 Prepare the pink tomato sauce as in the recipe for *Tortelloni di carciofi* on page 138.
4 Bring 4 quarts of water to a boil in a large saucepan or pot, add 1 tablespoon each of salt and of olive oil, and slide in the pasta using the kitchen towel it was spread out on.
5 When the sealed edges of the *tortelloni* are cooked *al dente*, drain and transfer to a serving dish. Pour the sauce over them and gently toss with the remaining grated cheese. Serve at once.

RAVIOLINI DI PESCE AL SUGO DI GAMBERI

Seafood Raviolini with Shrimp Sauce

INGREDIENTS

THE RAVIOLINI

2 Tbs butter
½ tsp fresh marjoram *or* ¼ tsp dried, finely chopped
½ lb bass *or* similar delicate white fish, boned and skinned
salt and freshly ground black pepper
¼ lb bay scallops
2 Tbs heavy cream
2 egg yolks
3 Tbs freshly grated parmigiano-reggiano cheese
pinch of freshly grated nutmeg
pasta dough made with 2 eggs (see page 36)

THE SAUCE

⅓ cup extra-virgin olive oil
3 whole garlic cloves, lightly crushed and peeled
2 Tbs tomato paste
½ cup dry white wine
½ lb medium shrimp, peeled and deveined if necessary
salt and freshly ground black pepper
1 cup heavy cream
2 Tbs finely chopped flat-leaf parsley

PREPARATION

THE RAVIOLINI

1 Put the butter in a skillet over a medium-high heat and allow it to foam. When the foam begins to subside, add the marjoram and the fish. Cook the fish on both sides, being careful not to overcook it or it will become dry: 4–6 minutes. Season with salt and black pepper and remove from the skillet using a slotted spoon.
2 Put the cooked fish in a food processor or blender, chop until almost creamy, then transfer to a mixing bowl.
3 Put the raw scallops in the processor or blender and chop them very finely. Add the cream and run the machine for about 5 more seconds. Transfer to the mixing bowl with the fish.
4 Add the egg yolks, grated cheese, and nutmeg to the mixture in the bowl. Combine thoroughly with a fork and taste for salt and black pepper.
5 Roll out the pasta dough as thinly as possible and make the stuffed *raviolini* as shown on page 43. Spread them out on a clean kitchen towel.

**Raviolini di pesce
al sugo di gamberi**

THE SAUCE

1 Put the olive oil and garlic in a skillet over a medium-high heat. When the garlic cloves have browned on all sides, remove and discard them. Remove the skillet from the heat.

2 Dissolve the tomato paste in the white wine, and pour into the skillet. Return it to a medium-high heat and reduce the wine by three-quarters.

3 Add two-thirds of the shrimp to the skillet. Cook, stirring, until they have turned pink: about 2–3 minutes. Season with salt and black pepper.

4 Turn off the heat under the skillet and remove the shrimp with a slotted spoon. Chop them very finely in a food processor, and return them to the skillet. Turn the heat to medium-high again and add half the cream. Cook, stirring often, until the cream has reduced by half. Remove from the heat.

5 Pour 4 quarts of water into a large saucepan or pot and place over a high heat.

6 Cut the remaining raw shrimp into thirds. Return the sauce to a medium-high heat and add the remaining cream and the cut raw shrimp. Cook, stirring frequently, until the newly added cream has reduced by half, then stir in the parsley. If the sauce appears to curdle at any point, it will correct itself if stirred well. Remove the skillet from the heat and set aside.

7 When the water for the pasta is boiling, add 1 tablespoon each of salt and of olive oil, and slide in the pasta from the kitchen towel.

8 When the sealed edges of the *raviolini* are cooked *al dente*, drain and transfer to a serving dish. Pour the sauce over them and gently toss until the pasta is evenly coated. Serve at once.

TORTELLONI DI CARCIOFI ALLA PANNA ROSA

Artichoke Tortelloni with Pink Tomato Sauce

INGREDIENTS

THE TORTELLONI

2 large or 3 medium artichokes
2 Tbs lemon juice
3 Tbs butter
3 Tbs finely chopped yellow onion
salt and freshly ground black pepper
1 egg yolk
½ cup freshly grated parmigiano-reggiano cheese
⅛ tsp freshly grated nutmeg
pasta dough made with 2 eggs (see page 36)

THE SAUCE

½ quantity of Burro e pomodoro sauce (see page 52), made in advance
½ cup heavy cream
¼ cup freshly grated parmigiano-reggiano cheese

PREPARATION

THE TORTELLONI

1 Trim the artichokes as shown on pages 126–7, slice thinly and place in a bowl of cold water with the lemon juice to prevent them from browning.
2 Melt the butter in a large skillet over a medium heat. Add the onion and cook until it softens and turns a rich golden color.
3 Drain the artichokes, rinse, and add to the skillet. Stir to coat well, season with salt and black pepper and pour in enough water to come ½ in up the side. Cook, uncovered, until the water has evaporated and the artichokes are very tender, adding more water if needed: 10–15 minutes.
4 Transfer to a food processor or blender and chop until creamy. Allow to cool in a mixing bowl.
5 Add the egg yolk, grated cheese, and nutmeg to the bowl. Mix thoroughly with a fork.
6 Roll out the pasta dough as thinly as possible and make the *tortelloni* as shown on page 42. Spread on a clean kitchen towel.

THE SAUCE

1 Pour 4 quarts of water into a large saucepan or pot and place over a high heat.
2 Pass the *Burro e pomodoro* sauce through a food mill then heat in a skillet over a medium-low heat until it begins to bubble.
3 Add the cream, raise the heat to medium and cook until the sauce is thick enough to coat a metal spoon: 2–3 minutes. Take off the heat.
4 When the water for the pasta is boiling, add 1 tablespoon each of salt and of olive oil, and slide in the pasta from the kitchen towel.

5 When the sealed edges of the *tortelloni* are cooked *al dente*, drain them and transfer to a serving dish. Pour the sauce and sprinkle the grated cheese over them, and gently toss until the pasta is evenly coated. Serve at once.

TORTELLI ALLA FERRARESE

Pasta Squares Filled with Sweet Potato

Tortelli *filled with sweet local pumpkin is a speciality of Ferrara in Emilia-Romagna. Outside Italy, orange-fleshed sweet potato is generally the best substitute for Italian pumpkin. The sauce I like best for these is butter and sage, but plain butter is good too.*

INGREDIENTS

THE TORTELLI

½ lb orange-fleshed sweet potatoes
vegetable oil for brushing
3 Tbs finely chopped prosciutto
1 egg yolk
1 cup freshly grated parmigiano-reggiano cheese
3 Tbs finely chopped flat-leaf parsley
⅛ tsp freshly grated nutmeg
salt and freshly ground black pepper
pasta dough made with 2 eggs (see page 36)

THE SAUCE

2 Tbs finely shredded fresh sage leaves (optional)
6 Tbs (¾ stick) butter, cut into small pieces
½ cup freshly grated parmigiano-reggiano cheese

PREPARATION

THE TORTELLI

1 Preheat the oven to 400°F.
2 Brush the sweet potatoes with vegetable oil and place them on a baking sheet in the oven. Cook until they are very tender and the skin feels as if it has separated from the flesh (cooking time will vary depending on the size of the potatoes). Remove the potatoes from the oven and peel as soon as they are cool enough to handle.
3 Pass them through a food mill or purée in a food processor. Allow to cool in a mixing bowl.
4 Add the *prosciutto*, egg yolk, grated cheese, parsley, and nutmeg, season with salt and black pepper, and mix thoroughly with a fork.

You can prepare the filling 1 day ahead and refrigerate it.

5 Roll out the pasta dough as thinly as possible and make the stuffed *tortelli* following the instructions given for *tortelloni* on page 42. Spread them out on a clean kitchen towel.

THE SAUCE

1 Pour 4 quarts of water into a large saucepan or pot and place over a high heat.

2 Melt the butter in a small saucepan over a medium heat. Season lightly with salt and black pepper. Either remove from the heat and set aside, or, if you are using sage, stir in the sage now, cook for 1–2 minutes longer until the butter just begins to darken, then set aside.

3 When the water for the pasta is boiling, add 1 tablespoon each of salt and of olive oil, and slide in the pasta from the kitchen towel.

4 When the sealed edges of the *tortelli* are cooked *al dente*, drain and transfer to a serving dish. Pour the sauce over them and gently toss until the pasta is coated, adding the grated cheese. Serve at once.

ROTOLO DI PASTA

Baked Sliced Pasta Roll Filled with Spinach

This elegant and delicious pasta dish comes from the Emilia-Romagna region of Italy and is a recipe I learned from my mother. It is perfect for a dinner party because you can prepare it ahead of time up to the point when it goes in the oven.

INGREDIENTS

THE ROTOLO

2lbs fresh spinach or 2 x 10oz packages frozen spinach, thawed
salt
4 Tbs (½ stick) butter
¼ cup finely chopped yellow onion
2oz finely chopped prosciutto
1 cup whole-milk ricotta
1¼ cups freshly grated parmigiano-reggiano cheese
pinch of freshly grated nutmeg
1 egg yolk
pasta dough made with 2 eggs (see page 36)

THE SAUCE

½ quantity of béchamel sauce (see page 142)
½ quantity of Burro e pomodoro sauce (see page 52), made in advance

PREPARATION

THE ROTOLO

1 If using fresh spinach, remove the stems and wash the leaves in several changes of cold water. Place them in a pan over a medium-high heat with ½ teaspoon of salt and just the water that clings to them after washing. Cover and cook until the leaves are tender: 8–12 minutes. If using frozen spinach, cook for about 3 minutes in enough

salted boiling water to cover. Drain and, when cool enough to handle, squeeze out the water and coarsely chop.

2 Melt the butter in a skillet over a medium heat. Add the onion and cook until it softens and turns a rich golden color. Stir in the *prosciutto* and sauté for 1 more minute. Add the spinach and sauté for another 3 minutes (do not worry if the spinach absorbs all the butter). Transfer to a mixing bowl and allow to cool.

3 Add the *ricotta*, 1 cup of the grated cheese, the nutmeg, and the egg yolk to the bowl. Mix with a fork, then knead with your hands to amalgamate the ingredients. Taste for salt and set aside.

4 Roll out the pasta dough, either by hand or through the pasta machine. Trim hand-rolled pasta into a rectangle of about 12 x 16in. If using machine-rolled pasta, lay three strips, approximately 16in long, side by side and slightly overlapping. Moisten the overlapping edges with water and seal them together.

5 Using a rubber spatula, spread the spinach filling over the pasta, no more than ⅛in deep. Leave ½in clear along the edges. Roll the pasta sheet and filling like a jelly roll, pinch the ends shut, then wrap it tightly in cheesecloth, tying the ends with string.

6 Bring 4 quarts of water to a boil in a large saucepan or pot, add 1 tablespoon of salt and gently immerse the pasta roll. Cook it at a steady boil for 20 minutes then lift it out carefully using two tongs or large spoons. Unwrap it, and allow it to cool.

TO ASSEMBLE AND BAKE

1 Make the béchamel sauce according to the recipe on page 142. Mix it with the *Burro e pomodoro* sauce.

2 Preheat the oven to 400°F, unless assembling the dish in advance to cook later.

3 Cut the cooled pasta roll with a sharp knife into ½in slices.

4 Spread a little of the béchamel and tomato mixture on the bottom of a shallow baking dish. Lay the pasta-roll slices on top, overlapping them like tiles if necessary.

5 Cover the pasta-roll slices with the rest of the béchamel and tomato mixture. Top with the remaining grated cheese.

 You may assemble the dish ahead of time up to this point and bake it later.

6 Place on the upper rack of the preheated oven. Bake for about 15–20 minutes or until a light crust forms on top. Remove from the oven and allow to rest for 10 minutes before serving.

Lasagne coi gamberi
e canestrelli
(page 142)

Rotolo di pasta
(page 139)

Tortelli alla ferrarese
with butter and sage sauce
(page 138)

Lasagne coi Gamberi e Canestrelli

Lasagne with Shrimp and Scallops

INGREDIENTS

3 Tbs extra-virgin olive oil
¼ cup finely chopped yellow onion
1 tsp finely chopped garlic
1 Tb finely chopped flat-leaf parsley
½ lb bay scallops, cut into ¼ in pieces
½ lb medium shrimp, peeled, deveined if necessary and cut into ¼ in pieces
salt and freshly ground black pepper
1 quantity of béchamel sauce (see right)
pasta dough made with 2 eggs (see page 36)

PREPARATION

1 Put the olive oil and onion in a skillet over a medium heat and cook until the onion softens and turns a rich golden color. Add the garlic and parsley and cook for about another minute.
2 Turn the heat up to medium-high and add the scallops. When they are no longer translucent, and any water they release has evaporated (about 1 minute), add the shrimp, season with salt and black pepper and cook until the shrimp turn pink. Remove the skillet from the heat.

TO ASSEMBLE AND BAKE

1 Make the béchamel sauce according to the recipe (see right).
2 Pour 4 quarts of water into a large saucepan or pot and place over a high heat. Place a large bowl filled with cold water, ice and a sprinkling of salt near the stove and spread out some clean, dry kitchen towels.
3 Roll out the pasta dough as thinly as possible. Cut it into strips 4in wide and shorter than the shallow baking dish you plan to use.
4 When the water is boiling, add 1 tablespoon of salt. Drop 4 pasta sheets at a time into the boiling water. Cook very briefly (about 1 minute), taking them out with a slotted spoon while still very *al dente* and placing them in the iced water. Swish about to remove excess starch, then lay the sheets in a single layer on the kitchen towels. Pat them dry. Continue until you have cooked all the pasta.
5 Preheat the oven to 400°F.
6 Smear the bottom of the baking dish with some of the béchamel sauce and mix the remainder with the seafood sauce. Line the bottom of the dish with a layer of pasta strips and spread just enough of the béchamel and seafood mixture over the pasta layer to cover it.

7 Continue layering the pasta and the sauce until there are at least 5 layers. Spread sauce thinly over the top layer of pasta.
8 Place on the upper rack of the oven. Bake for about 15 – 20 minutes or until a light golden crust forms on top. Remove from the oven and allow to rest for 10 minutes before serving.

Balsamella

Béchamel Sauce

INGREDIENTS

2 cups whole milk
4 Tbs (½ stick) butter
4 level Tbs all-purpose flour
salt and freshly ground black or white pepper

PREPARATION

1 Heat the milk until it just begins to bubble. Remove from the heat.
2 Meanwhile, melt the butter in a heavy-bottomed saucepan over a medium-low heat. Add the flour, mixing with a wire whisk until it is smooth. Let the mixture cook for 1 – 2 minutes, stirring constantly, and being careful not to let it brown.
3 Begin adding the hot milk, a few tablespoons at a time, whisking the mixture smooth before adding more. When the consistency becomes thinner you can begin adding milk more rapidly. Continue until all the milk has been mixed in.
4 Cook over a medium-low heat, stirring constantly with the whisk, until the sauce begins to thicken. The sauce is done when it coats the whisk thickly. Season with salt and black or white pepper before removing from the heat. Béchamel sauce is best when used the same day but it keeps overnight in the refrigerator if necessary.

LASAGNE ALLE ZUCCHINE

Lasagne with Zucchini

INGREDIENTS

*3lbs zucchini (if yellow zucchini are
available, use half green and half yellow)
2 Tbs extra-virgin olive oil
2 Tbs butter
1 tsp finely chopped garlic
1 Tb finely chopped flat-leaf parsley
½ tsp fresh thyme or ¼ tsp dried, finely chopped
salt and freshly ground black pepper
1½ quantities of béchamel sauce (see opposite)
⅛ tsp freshly grated nutmeg
¾ cup freshly grated parmigiano-reggiano cheese
pasta dough made with 2 eggs (see page 36)*

PREPARATION

1 Trim the zucchini and cut them in half lengthwise. Lay the halves cut-side down, and slice crosswise into ¼in semi-circles.
2 Put the olive oil, butter and garlic in a large skillet over a medium-high heat. When the garlic begins to change color, add the parsley and thyme and stir well.
3 Mix in the zucchini, season with salt and black pepper and continue cooking, stirring from time to time, until tender and lightly browned. Remove the zucchini and herb mixture using a slotted spoon and set it aside.
4 Make the béchamel sauce according to the recipe (see opposite). Pour about four-fifths of it into a bowl, add the zucchini and herb mixture, the nutmeg and ½ cup of the grated cheese, and stir.

TO ASSEMBLE AND BAKE

1 Roll out, cut and cook the pasta sheets, following the instructions for *Lasagne coi gamberi e canestrelli*, opposite (steps 2 to 4).
2 Preheat the oven to 400°F.
3 Smear the bottom of the baking dish with half the remaining béchamel sauce and cover with a layer of pasta. Cover the pasta with a thin layer of the béchamel and zucchini sauce.
4 Continue layering the pasta and the sauce until there are at least 5 layers. Spread the remaining béchamel and the remaining sauce over the top layer of pasta so that it is dotted with zucchini. Sprinkle the remaining ¼ cup of grated cheese on top.
5 Place on the upper rack of the oven. Bake for about 15–20 minutes or until a light golden crust forms on top. Remove from the oven and allow to rest for 10 minutes before serving.

LASAGNE ALLA BOLOGNESE

Lasagne with Meat Bolognese Sauce

INGREDIENTS

*1 quantity of Ragù sauce, made in advance
(see page 62)
1½ quantities of béchamel sauce (see opposite)
pasta dough made with 2 eggs (see page 36)
salt
⅔ cup freshly grated parmigiano-reggiano cheese
2 Tbs butter*

PREPARATION

1 Place the *ragù* in a mixing bowl.
2 Make the béchamel sauce according to the recipe (see opposite).

TO ASSEMBLE AND BAKE

1 Roll out, cut and cook the pasta sheets, following the instructions for *Lasagne coi gamberi e canestrelli*, opposite (steps 2 to 4).
2 Preheat the oven to 400°F (unless assembling the dish in advance to cook later).
3 Smear the bottom of a baking dish with some of the béchamel sauce and cover with a layer of pasta strips. Mix the rest of the béchamel with the meat sauce and spread a thin layer over the pasta.
4 Continue layering the pasta and the béchamel and meat sauce until there are at least 5 layers. Save enough sauce to thinly cover the top layer of pasta. Sprinkle the grated cheese on top and dot with the butter.

 You can assemble the dish ahead of time and refrigerate it for up to 2 days.

5 Place on the upper rack of the oven. Bake for about 15–20 minutes or until a light golden crust forms on top. Remove from the oven and allow to rest for 10 minutes before serving.

CANNELLONI ALLA SORRENTINA

Cannelloni Filled with Fresh Tomatoes, Mozzarella, and Basil

INGREDIENTS

2 Tbs butter
2 Tbs finely chopped yellow onion
1½ lbs fresh ripe plum tomatoes, peeled, seeded and cut into ¼ in dice
salt and freshly ground black pepper
2 Tbs shredded fresh basil
4oz fresh mozzarella
½ cup fresh whole-milk ricotta
½ quantity of béchamel sauce (see page 142)
pasta dough made with 2 eggs (see page 36)
¼ cup freshly grated parmigiano-reggiano cheese

PREPARATION

1 Melt the butter in a skillet over a medium heat. Add the onion and cook until it softens and turns a rich golden color.
2 Raise the heat to medium-high, add the tomatoes, season with salt and black pepper and cook until the tomatoes have reduced and separated from the butter: about 10–15 minutes.
3 Stir in the basil, cook for another 2 minutes then remove the skillet from the heat. Transfer the contents of the pan to a mixing bowl.
4 While the tomato and basil mixture is still warm, add the *mozzarella* and *ricotta*. Combine with a fork and taste for salt and pepper.

TO ASSEMBLE AND BAKE

1 Make the béchamel sauce according to the recipe (see page 142).
2 Preheat the oven to 400°F.
3 Roll out, cut and cook the pasta sheets, following the instructions given for *Cannelloni di carne* (see steps 3 to 5, opposite).
4 Spread a thin layer of the tomato and cheese filling over each rectangle, leaving a border of about ¼ in all around. Roll up the *cannelloni* in jelly-roll fashion.
5 Smear the bottom of a suitably sized baking dish with some béchamel sauce and arrange the *cannelloni* in a single layer (if necessary use two baking dishes). Cover the top of the *cannelloni* with the remaining béchamel, making sure all the pasta is well coated. Sprinkle the grated cheese on top.
6 Place on the upper rack of the oven. Bake for about 15–20 minutes or until a light golden crust forms on top. Remove from the oven and allow to rest for 10 minutes before serving.

CANNELLONI DI CARNE

Meat-Filled Cannelloni

These are a speciality of Lombardy in northern Italy. Preparing them is time-consuming but really quite simple. Cannelloni should not be tubes, but rectangles of homemade pasta spread with filling and rolled up. This recipe is essentially the way my mother makes them.

INGREDIENTS

4 Tbs (½ stick) butter
3 Tbs finely chopped yellow onion
¾ lb lean ground beef
salt and freshly ground black pepper
1 cup canned whole peeled tomatoes, with their juice, coarsely chopped
½ cup very finely chopped mortadella
1 egg yolk
⅛ tsp freshly grated nutmeg
1¼ cups whole-milk ricotta
1¼ cups freshly grated parmigiano-reggiano cheese
1 quantity of béchamel sauce (see page 142)
pasta dough made with 2 eggs (see page 36)

PREPARATION

1 Put 2 tablespoons of butter in each of two saucepans and melt over medium heat. Divide the onion between them and sauté to a rich golden color.
2 Add half of the ground beef to each saucepan and cook, crumbling the beef with a wooden

spoon, until the meat has lost its raw color. Add salt and black pepper.

3 Add the tomatoes to one of the pans and, as soon as they have started to bubble, reduce the heat to a mere simmer. Cook until the tomatoes have reduced and separated from the butter: about 35–45 minutes. (This is the meat sauce.)

4 Cook the meat in the other pan for just a few minutes after it has lost its raw color, then take it off the heat. Remove the meat from the pan using a slotted spoon and place in a mixing bowl.

5 When the meat in the mixing bowl has cooled completely, add the *mortadella*, egg yolk, nutmeg, *ricotta* and 1 cup of the grated cheese. Mix well with a fork. (This is the filling.)

 You can prepare the filling and the meat sauce 1 day ahead and refrigerate them.

TO ASSEMBLE AND BAKE

1 Make the béchamel sauce according to the recipe (see page 142), reducing the cooking time to achieve a thinner sauce.

2 Preheat the oven to 400°F.

3 Pour 4 quarts of water into a large saucepan or pot and place over a high heat. Place a large bowl filled with cold water, ice and a sprinkling of salt near the stove and spread out some clean, dry kitchen towels.

4 Roll out the pasta dough as thinly as possible and cut into rectangles of 3 x 5in.

5 When the water is boiling, add 1 tablespoon of salt and drop in as many rectangles of pasta as will comfortably float in the water. Cook very briefly (about 30 seconds), taking them out with a slotted spoon while still very *al dente* and placing them in the iced water. Once all the rectangles are cooked, swish them about in the iced water then remove them with a slotted spoon and place in a single layer on the kitchen towels. Pat them dry.

6 Add about 6 tablespoons of the béchamel to the filling, mixing it in well. Spread a thin layer of the filling over each rectangle, leaving a ¼in border all around. Roll up the *cannelloni* in jelly-roll fashion.

7 Smear the bottom of a suitably sized baking dish with some béchamel sauce and arrange the *cannelloni* in a single layer (if necessary use two baking dishes). Cover the top of the *cannelloni* with the meat sauce and the rest of the béchamel, making sure all the pasta is well coated. Sprinkle the remaining ¼ cup of grated cheese on top.

8 Place on the upper rack of the oven. Bake for about 15–20 minutes or until a light golden crust forms on top. Remove from the oven and allow to rest for 10 minutes before serving.

PIZZA DI MACCHERONI

Maccheroni "Pizza" with Tomatoes and Parmigiano-Reggiano Cheese

This unusual pasta dish is a speciality of the Principe restaurant in Pompei. It is meant to be eaten cold but I find it is also good warm.

INGREDIENTS

For 14oz *maccheroni*

¼ cup extra-virgin olive oil
½ tsp finely chopped garlic
1½ lbs fresh ripe plum tomatoes, peeled, seeded, and cut into ¼ in dice
salt and freshly ground black pepper
½ cup freshly grated parmigiano-reggiano cheese
2 eggs
2 Tbs butter

PREPARATION

1 Pour 4 quarts of water into a large saucepan or pot and place over a high heat.

2 Put the olive oil and garlic in a skillet over a medium-high heat and cook until the garlic begins to change color.

3 Add the tomatoes and cook until they have reduced and separated from the oil: 10–15 minutes. Season with salt and black pepper, remove from the heat and transfer to a mixing bowl large enough to accommodate the pasta later.

4 When the water for the pasta is boiling, add 1 tablespoon of salt and drop in the pasta all at once, stirring well.

5 When the pasta is *molto al dente* (about 1 minute away from being *al dente*), drain it and toss it in the bowl with the sauce. Mix in the grated cheese and allow the pasta to cool down.

6 Beat the eggs and mix them in with the pasta.

7 Melt the butter in a large nonstick skillet over a medium heat and allow it to foam. When the butter foam begins to subside, pour in the pasta mixture, pressing it down with a spoon until it is quite compact. Cook until the bottom forms a golden-brown crust.

8 Remove from the heat, place a large flat plate upside down over the pan, then turn the pan over, allowing the "pizza" to loosen on to the plate. You can allow the "pizza" to cool completely before serving, or try it lukewarm.

Also good with: *penne, elicoidali*

RIGATONI AL FORNO AI PORCINI

Baked Rigatoni with Porcini Mushrooms

INGREDIENTS

For 14oz rigatoni

1oz dried porcini
4 Tbs (½ stick) butter, plus extra for the baking dish
2 Tbs vegetable oil
⅓ cup finely chopped yellow onion
*½ cup canned whole peeled tomatoes, with their juice,
coarsely chopped*
1lb cremini or fresh white mushrooms, thinly sliced
2 Tbs finely chopped flat-leaf parsley
salt and freshly ground black pepper
⅔ quantity of béchamel sauce (see page 142)
⅓ cup freshly grated parmigiano-reggiano *cheese*

PREPARATION

1 Soak the dried *porcini* in a bowl with 1 cup
of lukewarm water for at least 20 minutes. Lift
them out, squeezing the excess water back
into the bowl, then rinse under cold running
water and coarsely chop them. Filter the water
they soaked in through a paper towel or a coffee
filter and set aside.
2 Put 3 tablespoons of the butter and all the oil
and onion in a large skillet over a medium heat and
sauté until the onion has softened and turned a
rich golden color. Add the tomatoes and the
reconstituted *porcini* with their filtered water.
Cook, stirring occasionally, until the liquid in the
pan has evaporated completely.
3 Raise the heat to medium-high, add the fresh
mushrooms and parsley and season with salt and
black pepper. Cook until all the water the mushrooms release has evaporated. Transfer to a bowl.
4 Make the béchamel sauce according to the
instructions (see page 142). Add to the mushroom
mixture in the bowl and mix in well.
5 Preheat the oven to 400°F.
6 Bring 4 quarts of water to a boil in a large
saucepan or pot, add 1 tablespoon of salt and drop
in the pasta all at once, stirring well.
7 When the pasta is *molto al dente* (about 1 minute
away from being *al dente*), drain it and toss it with
the sauce and 4 tablespoons of the grated cheese.
Transfer to a greased baking dish and top with the
remaining cheese and butter.
8 Place on the upper rack of the oven. Bake for
about 15–20 minutes or until a light golden crust
forms on top. Remove from the oven and allow to
rest for 10 minutes before serving.

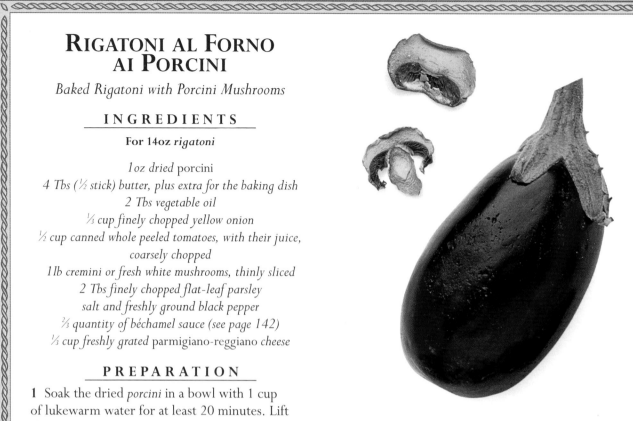

MACCHERONI AL FORNO ALLA RUSTICA

*Baked Maccheroni with Eggplant and
Smoked Mozzarella*

INGREDIENTS

For 14oz maccheroni

vegetable oil
1 large eggplant, peeled and cut into ¼in thick slices
salt
4 Tbs (½ stick) butter, plus extra for the baking dish
1 cup thinly sliced yellow onion
*1½ cups canned whole peeled tomatoes, with
their juice, coarsely chopped*
freshly ground black pepper
¼ cup freshly grated parmigiano-reggiano *cheese*
4oz Italian smoked mozzarella *(use fresh if smoked is
unavailable), very thinly sliced*

PREPARATION

1 Pour vegetable oil into a skillet until it comes
½in up the side. Place over a high heat. Once the
oil has become very hot, carefully slip in as many
slices of eggplant as will comfortably fit. As the
bottom of each slice turns golden brown, turn it
over, and when both sides are golden brown,
remove from the skillet and transfer to a plate
covered with paper towels. Continue frying until
all the eggplant is done. Sprinkle with salt.

2 Pour 4 quarts of water into a large saucepan or pot and place over a high heat.

3 Melt the butter in another skillet over a medium heat. Add the onion and cook until it softens and turns a rich golden color.

4 Add the tomatoes, season with salt and black pepper and cook until the tomatoes have reduced and separated from the butter. Remove the skillet from the heat and set aside.

5 Preheat the oven to 400°F.

6 When the water for the pasta is boiling, add 1 tablespoon of salt and drop in the pasta all at once, stirring well.

7 When the pasta is *molto al dente* (about 1 minute away from being *al dente*), drain and toss with the sauce and the grated *parmigiano-reggiano* cheese.

8 Smear the bottom of a shallow baking dish with butter and put in about half of the pasta, spreading it out evenly. Cover with all the eggplant slices and half the *mozzarella* slices. Put in the remaining pasta, and place the rest of the *mozzarella* slices on top.

9 Place on the upper rack of the oven. Bake for about 15–20 minutes or until a light golden crust forms on top. Remove from the oven and allow to rest for 10 minutes before serving.

Maccheroni al forno alla rustica

TORTA RICCIOLINA

Angel Hair Pasta and Almond Pie

This is a recipe my mother learned from a friend of ours, Margherita Simili, who is a fabulous Bolognese baker. The pie is intended to resemble noodles with Bolognese meat sauce – the cocoa-covered almond mixture representing the meat. The dessert is not simply an interesting conversation piece but an excellent moist pie, definitely worth making. The original recipe calls for candied citron, which I have never been very fond of, so I've substituted homemade candied oranges, which I find more appealing.

INGREDIENTS

CANDIED ORANGES

1 unpeeled orange, ends removed, cut in thin crosswise slices and seeds removed

⅓ cup granulated sugar, plus more as needed

PIE CRUST

1½ cups all-purpose flour

⅓ cup confectioner's sugar

salt

2 egg yolks

6 Tbs (¾ stick) butter, cut into small pieces and softened to room temperature, plus extra for the cake pan

FILLING

7oz blanched almonds

9 Tbs granulated sugar

1 tsp unsweetened, high quality cocoa

½ tsp grated lemon zest

pasta dough made with 2 eggs (see page 36)

8 Tbs (1 stick) butter

¼ cup dark rum

PREPARATION

CANDIED ORANGES

1 Put the orange slices, sugar and ¼ cup of water in a skillet large enough to fit them with minimum overlapping. Cook over a medium-low heat for about 15 – 20 minutes until the orange pith becomes translucent and tender, adding more water if necessary.

2 When the oranges are done, continue cooking until all the water has evaporated and the sugar has formed a thick syrup, coating the orange slices and giving them a glossy look.

3 Sprinkle sugar on a plate large enough to fit all the orange slices without overlapping (use 2 plates if necessary). Lay the slices on the sugar and cover them with more sugar. Allow to cool completely.

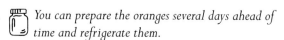 *You can prepare the oranges several days ahead of time and refrigerate them.*

PIE CRUST

1 Mix the flour, confectioner's sugar, and a tiny pinch of salt on a pastry board or work surface. Make a well in the center of the heaped mixture.

2 Put the egg yolks and butter in the well and work the flour into them, kneading into a smooth ball of dough. Wrap in plastic wrap and refrigerate for 1 hour.

TO ASSEMBLE AND BAKE

1 Put the almonds, orange slices, and granulated sugar in a food processor and chop to a medium-fine consistency. Transfer to a mixing bowl and add the cocoa and lemon zest, mixing well.

2 Preheat the oven to 375°F.

3 Lightly grease an 8in springform pan with butter, dust it with flour, and tap it upside down to remove any excess flour.

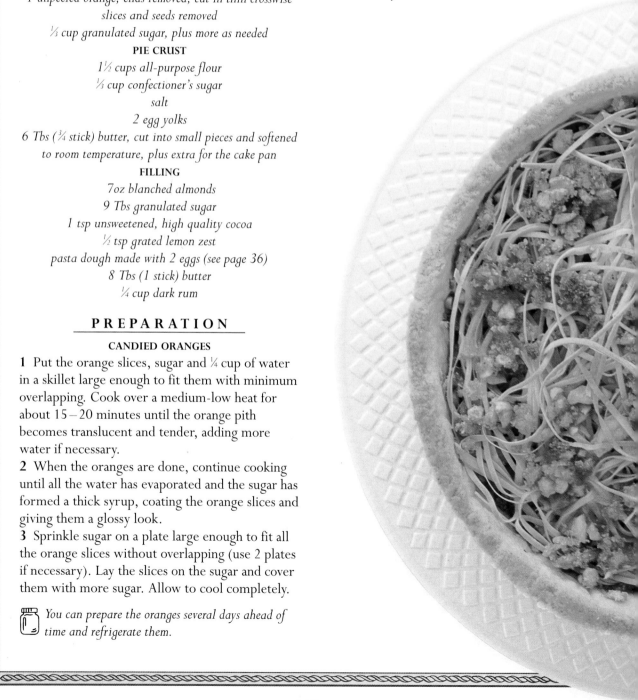

4 Dust the pastry board or work surface with flour and roll out the pastry into a large circle approximately ¼ in thick. Using the rolling pin, lift the pastry onto the springform pan, letting it drape over the bottom and the sides to line the pan. Trim the edges level with the top of the pan. (If the pastry breaks up, you can patch it together and it will still taste good.)

5 Roll out the pasta dough as thinly as possible. When it is dry enough, roll it up and cut it into the narrowest possible noodles (following the instructions on page 40). Fluff up the noodles to prevent them from sticking together and proceed quickly to the next step before they have a chance to dry out completely.

6 Put one-third of the noodles into the pan, leaving them fluffed up. Set aside 6 tablespoons of the almond mixture and sprinkle half of the remainder over the pasta. Dot with a third of the butter. Put in another third of the pasta, sprinkle the other half of the almond mixture on top and dot with another third of the butter. Add the remaining pasta, sprinkle the reserved almond mixture over it and dot with the remaining butter.

7 Place the pie on the top rack of the oven. After 15 minutes remove it from the oven and cover it with wax paper or aluminium foil. Return the pan to the oven and bake for 25 more minutes.

8 Take the pie out of the oven, remove the paper or foil and immediately sprinkle with the rum. Let it cool completely before serving. It will keep refrigerated for up to 10 days.

PREPARING VEGETABLES

These are the basic techniques for peeling, cutting, dicing, and chopping vegetables. When using a knife, choose one with a sharp blade. A dull blade requires the use of more force and consequently is harder to control. Keep your fingers bent away from the path of the knife.

CORING AND PEELING A FRESH BELL PEPPER

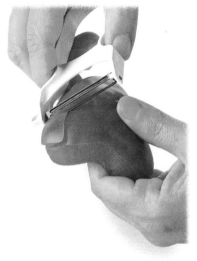

1 Slice the pepper in half along one of its ridges. With a circular movement, cut out the stem and core. Tap each half cut-side down to dislodge the seeds.·

2 Cut down the ridges of each pepper half. This enables you to cut away the pith and gives a smooth surface on which it easier to use the peeler.

3 Using a swivel-bladed peeler with a side-to-side sawing motion, peel the top of each piece, then remove the rest of the skin by peeling downward.

CUTTING A ZUCCHINI

1 Trim the ends of each zucchini and slice in half lengthwise. Place it cut-side down, and using the end of the blade, slice into long wedges.

2 Hold the wedges together and slice them crosswise into pieces. Rest the knife blade against your knuckles and bend your fingers away from the knife.

DICING A CARROT

1 Lay a peeled carrot flat on the cutting board and cut horizontally into three or four slices, depending on the thickness of the carrot.

2 Stack two or more of the slices and cut them into long thin sticks, holding the carrot with your fingers bent away from the knife.

3 Line up the sticks and slice them crosswise into small dice. Keep your fingers bent, with the flat of the blade against your knuckles.

PEELING AND SEEDING A TOMATO

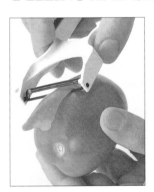

1 Peel the tomato using a swivel-bladed peeler. Use a side-to-side sawing motion at the same time as you peel downward.

2 Halve the tomato. Scoop out the seeds with your thumb and discard them. Coarsely chop the tomato flesh.

CHOPPING AN ONION

1 Trim each end of the onion and slice in half. Remove the skin. With the cut side down, slice lengthwise, leaving the root end intact.

2 Slice thinly crosswise until you reach the end that is intact. Chop up the last piece, then chop all the onion together as finely as necessary.

TIPS

• You can dice a stalk of celery in the same way as you would a carrot. First peel the outer part of the stalk to remove the tough strings. Flatten the stalk by pressing it down on the work surface with your hand.

• To dice a mushroom, remove the cap from the stem. Lay the cap flat on the cutting board and make two or three parallel cuts. Holding it together with your fingers, turn it a quarter turn and slice two or three more times. Cut the stem into pieces of the same size.

THE ITALIAN PANTRY

The ingredients on these pages are to be found in the well-stocked kitchen of any pasta-lover in Italy. If you build up a supply of these items, you will never be stuck for a quick and satisfying meal, and could even put together a feast at short notice. Store items in their original packaging, and if necessary transfer from pantry to refrigerator once opened.

SHORT-NOTICE MEALS

Aglio e olio (page 48)

Burro e pomodoro (page 52)

Pomodoro e basilico (page 54)

Arrabbiata (page 56)

Puttanesca (page 58)

Puttanesca bianca (page 89)

IN THE PANTRY

Most of these items keep for a long time and are used so often in Italian cooking that they will never go to waste. Keep them in stock along with a selection of your favorite dried pastas.

"OO" FLOUR

This flour is used in Bologna to make pasta. It may be difficult to find and you can use unbleached plain flour instead, which also produces very good results.

PORCINI

Fresh porcini are often hard to find but the dried versions are a readily available, flavorful alternative. They last forever, either in the original packaging or re-wrapped in plastic wrap. Look for packets with large slices of whole mushrooms and beware of lower-priced ones that are mostly stems.

GARLIC

Buy fresh, firm heads of garlic and store in a cool, dry place. They should stay fresh for about two weeks.

Capers packed in vinegar

Salted capers

CAPERS

Available in salt or wine vinegar. Salted ones have the purest flavor. Refrigerate them after opening.

ANCHOVIES

Look for flat fillets of anchovies in olive oil, in a can or a jar. Refrigerate them after opening.

NUTMEG

Buy nutmeg whole and grate it finely the moment you need it. Its flavor is powerful so use it sparingly.

JUNIPER BERRIES

Dry juniper berries (probably best known for making gin) have a unique flavor that is wonderfully suited to robust meats such as lamb.

RED PEPPER FLAKES

These are used for hot and spicy dishes and, in very small amounts, to liven up a dish without making it hot.

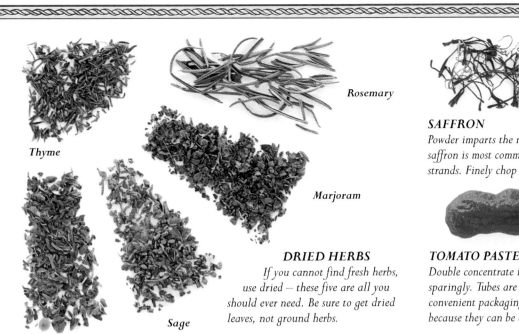

Thyme

Rosemary

Marjoram

Sage

Oregano

SAFFRON

Powder imparts the most flavor but saffron is most commonly available in strands. Finely chop strands before use.

DRIED HERBS

If you cannot find fresh herbs, use dried — these five are all you should ever need. Be sure to get dried leaves, not ground herbs.

TOMATO PASTE

Double concentrate is best, but use it sparingly. Tubes are the most convenient packaging for tomato paste because they can be easily resealed.

CANNED TOMATOES

The best are Italian plum tomatoes from San Marzano. Always use whole peeled tomatoes. They should have a fairly firm texture and a sweet ripe flavor without being too salty.

SUN-DRIED TOMATOES

These are available either dried or partly reconstituted in oil. If you buy the dried ones, soak them in water overnight, then squeeze out the excess water, and store them in olive oil.

BALSAMIC VINEGAR

True balsamic vinegar is at least 50 years old and exorbitant in price. For ordinary use, buy regular balsamic vinegar that is richly flavored, not too acid nor too sweet.

OLIVES

Italian and Greek black olives are the best to use. For green olives look for the large meaty southern Italian ones. Avoid pitted olives in cans or jars because they are usually quite bland.

OLIVE OIL

There are several grades of olive oil: extra-virgin is the highest grade and pure is the lowest. Extra-virgin oil is obtained from the first press of the olives and without the use of heat. I recommend using extra-virgin olive oil exclusively. The quality of all the ingredients you use is important in Italian cooking but olive oil is probably the one that makes the most difference in how well a dish turns out.

BASICS

Salt

Pepper

Onions

Dried bread crumbs

White wine

IN THE REFRIGERATOR

You don't need a great deal of space or money to have the basics on hand for a wide variety of pasta sauces. Buy the cheeses and the meat from a good Italian food store to be sure of having the real thing. Buy fresh herbs from a store that has a quick turnover.

BASIL

Keep this the same way as parsley. Wait until you are ready to use it before you tear or cut it because it quickly wilts and blackens.

PARSLEY

Flat-leaf parsley keeps in a jar of water in the refrigerator. Detach the leaves from the stems, wash and spin them dry before chopping.

BASICS
Milk
Heavy cream
Butter
Eggs
Carrots
Celery
Bell peppers

PARMIGIANO-REGGIANO

True parmigiano-reggiano *is a cheese of incomparable quality, flavor, and texture, which has been made in the same way for over 700 years. If you buy it in a big chunk, cut it into smaller pieces, wrap each tightly with plastic wrap and then with foil, store in the refrigerator and it will keep for several months. Use one piece at a time and grate it only just before serving.*

PECORINO ROMANO

This is a hard, sheep's milk cheese, aged for about one year, that is used for grating. It is sharper than parmigiano-reggiano, *so use it in smaller quantities. Stored like* parmigiano *it will also keep for a long time.*

RICOTTA

This is a cheese made from whey (the residue from the making of other cheeses) and it is creamy in texture and delicate in flavor. The best and creamiest is imported from Italy.

PLUM TOMATOES

The best plum tomatoes are ripe, red, and fairly firm. They are usually available all year round but are at their best in the summer. If using right away, do not refrigerate.

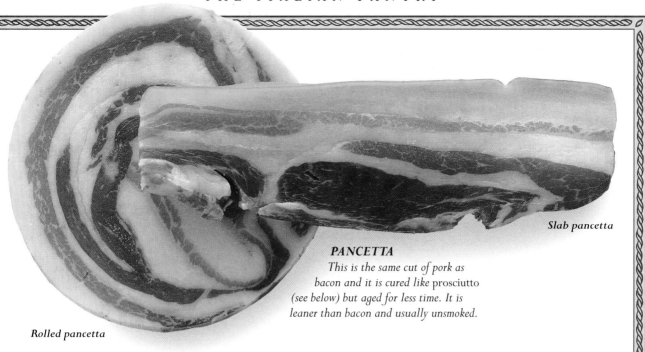

Slab pancetta

PANCETTA
*This is the same cut of pork as
bacon and it is cured like* prosciutto
*(see below) but aged for less time. It is
leaner than bacon and usually unsmoked.*

Rolled pancetta

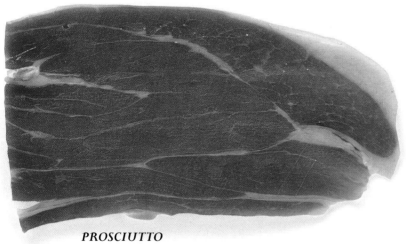

PROSCIUTTO
*This is an air- and salt-cured ham that is aged
for one year. If Italian* prosciutto *is not available
or is too expensive, look for a locally made
version that is rich in flavor and not too salty.*

SAUCES YOU CAN REFRIGERATE

Arrabbiata
(page 56)

Amatriciana
(page 84)

Boscaiola
(page 110)

Pollo
(page 112)

Salmone
(page 121)

Peperonata
(page 124)

IN THE FREEZER

Frozen spinach is useful to keep
on hand. It is quicker and easier
to use than fresh to make green
pasta and to combine with
ricotta for stuffings. Fresh
spinach is best for sauces.

When basil is plentiful, make
a large batch of *pesto* and freeze
it. The fresh leaves cannot be
frozen and thawed successfully.
You can also make your own

Italian-style sausage meat and
freeze it; see *Salsiccia di maiale*
on page 116.

Ragù and *Burro e pomodoro*
sauces freeze well. It is a good
idea to make more than you
need and freeze the rest as a
standby. Similarly with *Brodo*
(page 130): you are bound to
make more than you need at any
one time, so freeze the extra.

SAUCES YOU CAN FREEZE

Pesto di basilico
(page 50)

Burro e pomodoro
(page 52)

Ragù
(page 62)

Pomodoro
(page 88)

NOTES

AL DENTE, MOLTO AL DENTE

These terms, important in pasta cooking, translate literally as: "to the tooth" and "very much to the tooth." No Italian will cook pasta until it is soft and soggy: it is ready when it is still slightly firm and offers some resistance to the bite when you eat it. The stage of *molto al dente* comes around 30 to 90 seconds before *al dente* (depending on the pasta). Recipes ask for pasta to be *molto al dente* when it is not to be eaten immediately and will finish cooking either in the oven or in the pan.

GAS VS ELECTRIC STOVES

Gas stoves are almost always easier to use than electric. With gas, you get an immediate response when raising or lowering the heat and you have a visual gauge of its intensity. I have learned the hard way to deal with electric stoves. When you need to lower the heat, remove the pan from the heat source, adjust the temperature control, and wait about 30 seconds (waiting time will depend on the individual stove) before returning the pan to the heat. Because one stove's medium-high may be another's medium, use the heat levels in the recipes as an indication of what should be happening in the pan, rather than where to set the temperature control.

MEASUREMENTS

Cooking is not a scientific experiment where precise measurements are essential for a successful outcome. The quantities given in the recipes are a guide to the amounts and proportions of the various ingredients. Once you become familiar with a dish and the flavors of Italian cooking, it will not be necessary to measure every ingredient. You can sometimes make adjustments while cooking. If you chopped a little more onion or garlic than necessary, rather than discarding the excess, you sauté it a little less to reduce the intensity. Likewise, if you chopped too little, you can compensate by sautéing a little longer.

OILS

Occasionally a recipe calls for vegetable oil instead of olive oil. Olive oil is used wherever it contributes to the flavor of the dish, but when its only function would be to prevent butter from burning during frying, vegetable oil is adequate. There is no point in wasting good-quality extra-virgin olive oil.

PARMESAN
PARMIGIANO-REGGIANO

Parmesan is a general name for a type of Italian cheese of which the original and best is *parmigiano-reggiano*. The production of true *parmigiano-reggiano* is limited by law to a relatively small area in the region of Emilia-Romagna, whose environment accounts for the particular flavor of its milk. The method of production is also regulated by law and each wheel of cheese, which must be aged a minimum of 18 months before being sold, is inspected before it receives the stamp of approval on its side. The best way to buy the cheese is in chunks taken straight from the wheel, whose stamp of approval is visible. Avoid Parmesan in packets, especially ready grated.

SALT

Although I have not indicated amounts for salt in the recipes, it should not be considered an optional ingredient (except, of course, for sound medical reasons). Salt is essential in bringing out the flavor of food and a properly salted dish will be rich in flavor without tasting salty. You can test this by taking two glasses of wine and putting a little salt into one. Smell the wine and you will notice how much fuller and more intense the one with salt smells.

SAUCEPAN SIZE

You need a generously sized saucepan or pot for cooking pasta. It should accommodate all the water required for the quantity of pasta (see page 45) and still have room for the water to bubble up and the pasta to move around. Stir occasionally while cooking to prevent the pasta from sticking. You don't need olive oil except when cooking stuffed pasta.

TIMING

If in any doubt over how long a sauce will take to cook, finish it before you start the pasta. Pasta does not take long to cook, and should never be overcooked, while a sauce can be reheated, or cooked slowly at the end. Pasta must be tossed with sauce the moment it is drained.

INDEX

Figures in **bold** refer to pages with illustrations

ACKNOWLEDGMENTS

Author's appreciation

First and foremost, my parents, Victor and Marcella Hazan. I could not have written this book without their inspiration, support and all that they have taught me through the years.

My wife, Polly, for her love, her excellent palate which was invaluable when I was testing recipes, and her proofing and coaching of my prose.

Jenifer Lang, for recommending me to DK for this project.

Robert Lescher, for his encouragement and confidence in me.

Mari Roberts, Tracey Clarke, Carolyn Ryden and all the staff at DK in London for their excellent work in putting together this book and their patience with me; Lyn Rutherford for producing the dishes for photography; Clive Streeter and Amanda Heywood for their beautiful photographs; Pamela Thomas, Jeanette Mall, Julee Binder and the staff at DK in New York for all their help and support.

Christy McCartney and Leroy Kunert for testing my recipes; the staff at Perlina Restaurant in Portland, Oregon for giving me ideas for some of the recipes in this book; Alberto Consiglio's book, *I Maccheroni*, which describes the legend of Chico, the Neapolitan magician.

And last, but not least, all the chefs and cooks I have had the fortune of meeting in my travels in Italy.

Dorling Kindersley would like to thank Lyn Rutherford for preparing the food that appears throughout the book; Meg Jansz for preparing food on pages 135, 140–1, 147, 148–9; Steve Gorton for additional photography (pages 2, 3, 4, 5, 6); Steven Begleiter and Dirk Kaufman for the photographs on pages 7 and 8; Sarah Ponder for the artworks; Alexa Staće for editorial assistance; Hilary Guy for styling pages 32–3 and 70–1; Sarah Ereira for the index; Carluccio's of Neal Street, London and Mauro's, Muswell Hill Broadway, London for fresh pasta for catalog photography; and Patricia Roberts and Frederick Hervey-Bathurst for additional props.